TECHNOLOGY AT THE MARGINS

TECHNOLOGY AT THE MARGINS

How IT Meets the Needs of Emerging Markets

SAILESH CHUTANI
JESSICA ROTHENBERG AALAMI
AKHTAR BADSHAH

WILEY

John Wiley & Sons, Inc.

Published by John Wiley & Sons, Inc., Hoboken, New Jersey.
Published simultaneously in Canada.

Limit of Liability/Disclaimer of Warranty: While the publisher and author have used their best efforts in preparing this book, they make no representations or warranties with respect to the accuracy or completeness of the contents of this book and specifically disclaim any implied warranties of merchantability or fitness for a particular purpose. No warranty may be created or extended by sales representatives or written sales materials. The advice and strategies contained herein may not be suitable for your situation. You should consult with a professional where appropriate. Neither the publisher nor author shall be liable for any loss of profit or any other commercial damages, including but not limited to special, incidental, consequential, or other damages.

For general information on our other products and services or for technical support, please contact our Customer Care Department within the United States at (800) 762-2974, outside the United States at (317) 572-3993 or fax (317) 572-4002.

Wiley also publishes its books in a variety of electronic formats. Some content that appears in print may not be available in electronic books. For more information about Wiley products, visit our web site at www.wiley.com.

Library of Congress Cataloging-in-Publication Data:
Chutani, Sailesh, 1964–
    Technology at the margins : how IT meets the needs of emerging markets/Sailesh Chutani, Jessica Rothenberg Aalami, Akhtar Badshah.
        p. cm. —(Microsoft executive leadership series; 22)
    Includes index.
    ISBN 978-0-470-63997-9 (hardback); ISBN 978-0-470-92063-3 (ebk);
    ISBN 978-0-470-92064-0 (ebk); ISBN 978-047-0-92065-7 (ebk)
    1. Information technology.   2. New products.   I. Aalami, Jessica Rothenberg, 1972–
II. Badshah, Akhtar.   III. Title.
    T58.5.C46 2010
    658.4'038—dc22

                                                                    2010023275

Printed in the United States of America

10 9 8 7 6 5 4 3 2 1

ABOUT THE EXECUTIVE LEADERSHIP SERIES

The Microsoft Executive Leadership Series is pleased to present independent perspectives from some of today's leading thinkers on the ways that IT innovations are transforming how organizations operate and how people work. The role of information technology in business, society, and our lives continues to increase, creating new challenges and opportunities for organizations of all types. The titles in this series are aimed at business leaders, policymakers, and anyone interested in the larger strategic questions that arise from the convergence of people, communication media, business process, and software.

Microsoft is supporting this series to promote richer discussions around technology and business issues. We hope that each title in the series contributes to a greater understanding of the complex uncertainties facing organizations operating in a fast-changing and deeply connected new world of work, and is useful in the internal dialogues that every business conducts as it plans for the future. It remains our privilege and our commitment to be part of those conversations.

Titles in the Executive Leadership Series:

CONTENTS

FOREWORD

During the late 1990s, at the height of the digital divide debate, I saw the power of information technology (IT) and launched many IT companies, including Grameen Phone, in Bangladesh. I believed then, and continue to believe today, that information technology has a role to play in accelerating the pace of change and providing unique opportunities to people struggling to come out of poverty. I also believe that through the use of information technology we will be able to help the poor to come out of poverty with their own efforts. I have seen this firsthand through my work at Grameen; I have seen how cell phones have impacted the lives of the poor. IT has created new business opportunities for the poor, as well as connecting illiterate rural women with the world at large.

Over the last five years I have been focusing on the important role of business—particularly social business—in creating a world without poverty. I believe that the future of capitalism lies in harnessing the power of the free market to solve the problems of poverty, hunger, and inequality. For me, this book addresses the heart of the problem we face in creating a world without poverty. It makes a convincing argument that if innovators, development experts, and business leaders reimagine their respective roles and forge new partnerships, they can have a broad impact on society by building businesses that are sustainable and that improve lives. Through such collaborations, businesses would be able to reach nontraditional markets while the innovators and NGOs would see their successful experiments touch millions.

Today, few doubt that IT can play a fundamental role in helping underserved communities not only gain access to much-needed information and knowledge, but also create new and viable businesses to reach customers all over the world. However, the specific role of technology is not always clear in people's minds. The decision makers need a framework to think about these issues, to distinguish problems that require research from those that require a business model or scaling up, and to base their decisions on what is known from empirical evidence. In *Technology at the Margins: How IT Meets the Needs of Emerging Markets,* the authors admirably meet that need. They provide a structured framework to evaluate the key problems in health care, education, microfinance, and the environment, and show which ones can be addressed through technical innovation, business model innovation, and creative partnerships between the public and private sectors. Through their examples they show that even the existing information technology can be used effectively to address the most pressing needs of humanity in education, health, finance, and the environment. They also argue that innovation targeted at meeting the needs of those at the bottom of the pyramid is difficult but can yield big dividends if successful.

I have known Dr. Badshah for over two decades, when he was at MIT, at Digital Partners, and now at Microsoft, and have been impressed by the depth of his knowledge and his dedication to development issues through technology. I first met Dr. Chutani in 2007 when he showed me research prototypes at Microsoft Research that demonstrated how phone-based technologies could improve access and affordability of health care—something that is of deep interest to Bangladesh and to me. I am delighted to see that he has decided to apply these ideas to the real world situation. Together, these three authors have created a compelling book that is a must-read for those who are looking at creating a world without poverty through sustainable businesses.

Professor Muhammad Yunus
Nobel Peace Prize Winner,
2006, and Founder of the
Grameen Bank and other
Grameen companies

PREFACE

Although the three authors of this book each bring different yet complementary backgrounds and experiences, they share a great belief that information technology can make a difference in social and economic development. Sailesh is an engineer, scientist, and entrepreneur by training and profession; Akhtar is an architect, educator, and social entrepreneur; and Jessica is an economic geographer, development expert, and advisor. Each has arrived in this field through a unique set of experiences and looks at the world through a different set of lenses. This book is a reflection of our combined yet varied viewpoint, which we hope makes it exciting and interesting reading. Sailesh and Akhtar both grew up in India and studied and lived in Switzerland and the United States at different times: Akhtar was in Zurich in 1980 for a four-month stint while Sailesh lived a few years in Lausanne. Jessica, however, grew up and studied in California, undertaking travels in Europe, Asia, and elsewhere as part of her global research and practice.

In March 2004, Sailesh decided to uproot his family from the San Francisco Bay Area to move to Redmond, Washington, much to the shock and surprise of his friends and colleagues, who viewed him as a diehard Californian. He was, of course, following the long line of people who had been seduced by the possibility of being at Microsoft and utilizing its great resources to try to change the world. He was also looking forward to working with Rick Rashid, Dan Ling, and Kevin Schofield, all very well known in computing research, who had recruited him into Microsoft Research, one of the foremost research labs in the world. Akhtar, however, moved from the field of architecture to development and started a non-profit in Seattle focusing on the role of information technology and development. He also joined Microsoft in March 2004 to run Microsoft's Community Affairs and philanthropy program.

After a decade of research and travel to better understand global production networks and sustainable development issues, Jessica started her research and consulting work with Microsoft in 2005 to help explore emerging market opportunities—from both business and community investment viewpoints. She and her teams have worked across the company, spanning research, product and business development, and community affairs, at U.S. headquarters and subsidiaries in East and Southeast Asia, the Middle East, and Africa, and in the field, where pilots and programs were running in over 30 countries.

Sailesh's role at Microsoft was to identify emerging technologies and trends before they became commonplace and to harness them to start new businesses and products for Microsoft. He decided to do so by collaborating with the top research scientists in the world who were working in universities and government research labs. Since these scientists are not constrained by meeting quarterly revenue numbers, they are more likely to ask fundamental questions and stay with them long enough to make interesting discoveries. And they also tend to be very cost effective by relying extensively on graduate students.

To discover what these scientists found interesting and what kind of collaboration they would look for with Microsoft, Sailesh went around the world and asked them. A pattern emerged very quickly. Yes, scientists were asking fundamental questions about computing and its novel applications and they wanted collaboration, financial resources, and technologies from Microsoft to help them. But some of them, notably a small number of research labs at the University of California at Berkeley, Carnegie Mellon University, Stanford, and the University of Washington, among others, were also being driven to explore information and communication technology (ICT) to solve the problems of development and poverty, particularly in the case of the countries of Latin America and South East Asia, and especially India.

Akhtar's role, however, was to bring his expertise in the field to bear on development and to manage Microsoft's global philanthropic efforts focused on bringing the benefits of information technology to underserved communities all over the world. He, too, traveled the world to learn from the hundreds of projects Microsoft supported in small, large, rural, and urban communities so that youth, women, the elderly, and the disabled could learn basic information technology skills and achieve social and economic empowerment.

By the time of the publication of this book, Akhtar will have spent over a decade studying and investing in projects at the bottom of the economic pyramid, first with Digital Partners (the nonprofit that he established), and then with Microsoft. It was quite a shock at first to see that the world's poor (those living on less than $2 a day) could benefit from information technology, especially in the early part of this decade. At the end of this decade, as we reflect in this book, we are seeing not just an embrace of technology but innovation specifically targeted to benefit poor segments of society.

Jessica also spent the same part of the decade researching how information technology can bring about positive change in societies and how corporations and governments can play a role to foster that change. Going between these agents, she focused on the potential social and economic impact that relevant technologies may have on emerging economies via innovative entrepreneurs. Her workshops over the years in Asia (including the Middle East) and Africa on ICT for Education, Health, Microbusiness, and Development were aimed at empowering practitioners, managers, and partners to take advantage of the often unexpected and exciting ways information technology has benefited individuals and societies. She shares many of those examples here.

Each of us became aware that the elite in the countries that we visited felt that the ICT revolution has largely bypassed those at the bottom of the pyramid. This was especially stark in countries, such as India, which had become global software powerhouses but built very few ICT products or services for their own populations. These academic and policy elite felt that if the technologies were constructed to meet the specific needs of those at the bottom of the pyramid, it could enrich and empower them in the same way as it had done for those living in the developed and the affluent world. Of course, first some serious research questions had to be answered to determine what kind of ICT would be affordable, accessible, and relevant for that constituency. There was just one problem: No money was available to fund that research.

The funding agencies and most of the scientists either were not aware of the problems or did not think that the problems were substantive or interesting and didn't consider the line of inquiry to be legitimate. And there were no conferences or journals to publish that research, either. To be fair, it was not clear what were the right questions to ask and whether these were in the realm of computer science, sociology, economics, anthropology, or a completely new field! This was one of the areas where academic researchers were looking for help from Microsoft. Microsoft could not only provide seed funding for the initial research, but it could also legitimize the area in the eyes of other scientists and hence attract more talent and resources to the problem.

In order for Microsoft to be involved in this space, there had to be a business rationale. As we started to think through the problem, a couple of fortunate developments took place. Sailesh and Akhtar were introduced and Akhtar in turn introduced Jessica, who also had looked at the problem of ICTs and development very deeply over the years.

Through our conversations over the next several years, we were also introduced to C. K. Prahalad and his work on the market represented by those at the bottom of the pyramid. His recent passing is a remarkable loss, but his legacy remains, an indelible mark on the field. Our work, too, is inspired and influenced by our interactions with other colleagues in the field. Sailesh was also becoming convinced that the next generation of disruptive innovation could come out of emerging markets, as local entrepreneurs tried to meet the needs of those at the bottom of the economic pyramid. This is something that Prahalad had not postulated, but was hard to miss in one industry after another—be it solar, wind, or telecommunications, and now computing. In our minds, all the pieces were in place.

Being at Microsoft has its advantages as there are a number of people with similar interests and we could bounce ideas off these folks. Another advantage is the opportunity to collaborate among different groups and try out something new and innovative. Microsoft had a perfect tool for that, called the "Thinkweek." Twice a year, anyone in Microsoft could submit ideas to Bill Gates, who is referred to in Microsoft by his email alias, BillG. BillG would take off for a week and read all those ideas and provide extensive and pointed feedback on some of them. An endorsement or support from him could be an important boost to build support in the company.

Sailesh did just that. He submitted a paper whose main premise was that Microsoft's business could be disrupted by innovations coming out of the emerging markets, especially those innovations that tried to make computing more affordable and accessible at very low price points. Sailesh further argued that our best bet against being surprised by those innovations was to set up groups in those markets to pursue these innovations ourselves. BillG was intrigued and gave extensive comments but asked whether we had ideas on the form that such affordable computing could take. We didn't, but decided to find out.

We had come to know of Uday Desai's work on cell phones. He is a professor at Indian Institute of Technology (IIT) Bombay who pioneered cell phone–based services for the poorer segments of India. We ran a small program to find out if there were others in India working on similar problems of making ICT more useful for those at the bottom of the pyramid. There were. Many labs were exploring ways to reduce the cost of bringing the Internet to villages by using mesh networking. Others were using a phone-based system to issue flood warnings; yet others were going after the illiteracy problem by using PC-based kiosks. It was possible that India was representative of a worldwide phenomenon. We decided to run a worldwide request for proposals (RFP) to invite ideas on how to make ICT more affordable, accessible, and relevant to those at the bottom of the pyramid.

The RFP promised small grants of up to $100,000 as seed funds for a total of just over $1 million and access to Microsoft technologies and resources. Sailesh and Akhtar collaborated on this RFP and proposed adding the criterion that each researcher have a nongovernmental organization (NGO) partner in the field, so that their research would be informed by cultural as well as pragmatic context. In hindsight, that proved to be a great approach. We were, of course, concerned whether anyone would submit proposals and whether the proposals were going to be along the lines we envisioned. Our concerns proved to be completely misplaced. The RFP was oversubscribed by ten times. We received more than 160 high-quality proposals from around the world. John Sangiovanni and Tom Healy, the two program managers who managed the program, got swamped. They had to engage additional help from the research and product groups to review the proposals. We selected 16 proposals to fund.

Suddenly, we had a community of researchers and a glimpse into what the answers could look like. Akhtar and Sailesh also decided to fund the online version of a journal, *ITID* (*Information Technology and International Development*), and the ICTD conference in collaboration with University of California, Berkeley, and Microsoft Research (MSR) India, in order to have a venue where the results from that RFP could be published. All that was needed now was patience and care and management of the collaborations with the RFP winners. Today, both the journal and the conference are major venues where researchers are able to publish and share their work.

Around the same time, Kentaro Toyama, a researcher in MSR, moved to India to help his manager and a fellow researcher, P. Anandan, set up the India lab. He decided to create a multidisciplinary group to explore how ICT could be used to help with the problem of development. This group was based in India and had a very important focus on fieldwork. Now we had an internal group of experts to work with as well! In parallel, a grassroots effort emerged to convince Microsoft to make products specifically targeted for the emerging markets and for those at the bottom of the pyramid. BillG sanctioned the creation of such a group, which was aptly named the "Unlimited Potential Group." This meant that we had business customers for the results coming out of our program as well as those from Kentaro's group.

Over the following year, we learned a tremendous amount about the problems as well as potential solutions while working with the RFP winners and others. It became clear that the cell phone was the affordable and accessible "computing" platform for the masses. These devices were becoming as powerful as the PCs of a few years ago. Most people, even those who were illiterate, could easily learn to use them. They could be recharged even in the absence of an electric grid. They didn't require expensive and complicated maintenance, and most importantly, they were becoming very cheap, extremely fast. This meant that even the poorest people could begin to afford them, especially with the advent of the prepaid plans and extremely low tariffs. It also became clear that the cell phones were not being used as computers and much work remained to be done.

We did discover, however, that what people were looking for from ICT once affordability and accessibility were addressed was help with improving their earning potential and access to credit, access to health care, and education for their children. They also saw the potential for making their voices heard in civic matters.

We decided to go deeper in the health-care space since ICT was already beginning to play a role in commercial microlending. We ran another RFP in 2007 that specifically targeted using the cell phone as a platform for health care, to make health care more affordable and accessible. Just like the first RFP, we were the first to fund this kind of work and to take a risk on what seemed like science fiction to most people. Tom Healy and Kris Tolle managed that program. As before, the response was tremendous, but we were better prepared. We selected a dozen or so projects to fund out of nearly 100 submissions. Kris and Tom continue to cultivate those collaborations.

In addition, we used our collaboration with the FAPESP (Fundação de Amparo à Pesquisa do Estado de São Paulo) of Brazil to explore projects specific to Brazil, and our Latin America Virtual Research Institute to explore projects that were relevant to Latin America. These programs were managed by Jaime Puente and Juliana Salles, both of whom have roots in Latin America but have lived and worked in the United States as well.

Some of these projects are transitioning from research to products today, and some are attracting the attention of foundations and NGOs and winning global recognition. Today, the field of mobile technologies for health care (or mHealth) has become one of the hottest trends in health care globally, fueled by the desire to save costs in health-care systems around the world and to bring care to those who don't have it today. It is attracting venture capital as well as foundation money. The United Nations and Vodafone Foundations commissioned a special report on mHealth for Development, which included many of the projects funded by our two RFPs and others that we funded over the years. Well-established players are thinking through their own mHealth strategies or buying companies that have them. The National Institutes of Health hosted its first mHealth Summit as a prelude to more substantive funding in the area. The Gates Foundation has announced similar programs as well, including it in one of its grand challenge topics. Sailesh started an mHealth company, Mobisante, Inc., to pursue this field full time. If Mobisante is successful, it will make ultrasound imaging dramatically more affordable and accessible both in the United States as well as in the emerging markets.

Similar developments are taking place in finance and education. Furthermore, many of the pioneering companies are coming out of emerging economies, such as M-Pesa, SELCO, and KickStart, to name a few. These trends have taken on lives of their own, beyond Microsoft, beyond one company, industry, or country, and have become truly global in their impact. And it is just the beginning, with some important lessons to share and learn along the way. As a research activity, it has gained respect within the computer science field as the mainstream publications start to feature research in this area. The last two Information and Communications Technology and Development (ICTD) conferences have attracted thousands of participants and very strong research results, and keynote speakers such as Bill Gates.

However, it is not yet clear whether these experiments will become sustainable businesses, whether multinational corporations (MNCs) or the local companies would dominate, and whether the real impact will have to await new inventions in the future or whether the current technology is good enough. As Akhtar and Sailesh talked with Jessica, it became obvious to us that there was a need out there to give the decision makers a framework to think about these issues, to distinguish problems that require research from those that require a business model or scaling up, and to base this framework on what had been tried, what works, and what doesn't. That is what we have set out to do in this book.

Numerous people have influenced our work, from our colleagues at Microsoft and in academia to business and nonbusiness circles that have graciously shared their ideas, helped us to consider other viewpoints, and provided honest and constructive feedback on our work. Special thanks are due to Karen Speerstra, Dr. Mahad Ibrahim, Dr. Jaspal Sandhu, Dr. Joyojeet Pal, and Jennifer Johnson for their support and input over the course of writing this book. Most importantly, this project would not have been possible had it not been for our time in the field where many of the projects we cite have been implemented. If it were not for the project partners, practitioners, and participants—from young people, women, and farmers to community leaders, all living in underserved communities around the world—we would not have had lessons to share. Finally, we want to thank our families for allowing us the time to write, travel, and reflect in order to tell this story—and ultimately write this book.

CHAPTER 1

INFORMATION AND COMMUNICATION TECHNOLOGIES FOR EVERYONE

INNOVATIVE WAYS TO REACH THE MAJORITY OF THE WORLD

Information and communication technologies (ICTs) have revolutionized our lives by changing the ways we live, play, work, communicate, learn, manage our finances, and stay healthy. But for people living in the poorer areas of our planet—usually areas with insufficient infrastructure, environmental challenges, weak governance, and few resources—this is not the case. The majority of the world's people—the four billion at the bottom of the global economic pyramid—remain largely unable to capitalize on the ICT revolution.

Why? There are many reasons, but the primary ones are:

- Technology is usually not affordable; it's too expensive in relation to their purchasing power.

- Technology is often not relevant to their needs.
- Technology may not be accessible because the context in which it was designed—for a literate, affluent, educated population—is very different.

What if we could change all this? What if ICTs were affordable, relevant, and accessible? What impact would that have on reducing poverty and improving lives? What barriers need to be overcome before that can happen? What innovation is required?

A COMPUTER FOR EVERY CHILD—A GREAT IDEA, BUT . . .[1]

The vision of One Laptop per Child (OLPC) generated significant enthusiasm. It was seductive to imagine solving the world's education problems by giving an inexpensive $100 PC to every child. However, the impact fell short of the lofty expectations. The cost, low by developed countries' standards, still represented a big fraction of the annual income of the target audience. It was still a PC, which meant it needed a usable electric grid, which is unreliable in most developing countries. It also needed literate people to use it, which made it inaccessible to more than 40 percent of the population in some countries. Furthermore, these machines are sophisticated and powerful, and require high expertise to maintain and service them, which was another missing element. And most important, the magic of hardware comes to life through great software. Since the purchasing power of this group was perceived as low, vendors did not invest in creating compelling software applications for them, further reducing the case for buying the laptops.

After many years and millions of dollars of investment by the countries least able to afford it, the outcomes have fallen short of the expectations. Few machines were built and sold. The ones that were built will probably face a limited future since there is no ecosystem and capacity to repair and maintain them. The impact, such as it was, was instead felt in developed economies where the specter of OLPC forced PC makers to reduce costs and come out with a new and competitive category of Netbooks.

What partnerships need to be forged? Are there lessons from other arenas such as consumer products that might be applied? What could multinational corporations (MNCs), nongovernmental organizations (NGOs), governments, and most important, individual entrepreneurs do to facilitate the process?

These are some of the questions and possible solutions we explore in this book, drawing from actual successes and failures from the field.

What Are the Needs of This Group?

> *Poverty is more than just a lack of money—it is a lack of opportunity, rights, and resources. It is created by ill health and poor or no health care, inadequate housing and transportation, illiteracy, and racial and gender discrimination. It can be affected by things as personal as one's actions and as uncontrollable as the weather. Poverty is caused by things as small as lacking a few dollars of credit and as large as war, national debt and international trade policies.*
> —*Shannon Daley-Harris, Jeffrey Keenan, and Karen Speerstra,* Our Day to End Poverty

Every day, facts wash into our minds and seep out again nearly as quickly. Throughout this book, we've highlighted some of the facts you might wish to remember. But one fact that has been bandied about for the past few years bears considering here: *Nearly half of the world lives on less than $2 a day.* They live on today's food, today's energy, today's clothing, and today's chances of staying alive.

They need to augment their meager incomes. They need to provide food and shelter. They need to take care of their health and the health of their children. They need to educate their families and learn more themselves. They need to learn to survive in a world short of resources and becoming more constrained each day.

But as we learned from *The Next 4 Billion*,[2] there are still four billion consumers. They buy things, albeit usually at much higher cost than need be.

People at the base of the economic pyramid are customers with the power to choose—not simply "beneficiaries."
—Ashish Karamchandani, Michael Kubzansky, and Paul Frandano, "Emerging Markets, Emerging Models"

Billions of consumers will be reached only by using innovative techniques and different business models from the ones in use in the rest of the world. As Prahalad and Hammond have said, "to reach them, CEOs must shed old concepts of marketing, distribution and research."[3]

Can ICT Really Help?

Yes it can—by reducing transaction costs and by reducing the level of skills required to deliver services. Take, for example, efforts to provide health-care services at a fraction of the cost of similar services in the developed world.

As Figure 1.1 illustrates, costs of health-care services provided are largely determined by the location where those services are provided and by the skill level of the person providing those services.[4]

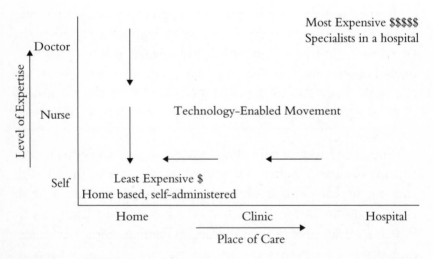

Figure 1.1   Impact of ICT on Health Care

Source: Adapted from Clayton Christensen, Jerome H. Grossman, and Jason Hwang, *The Innovator's Prescription: A Disruptive Solution for Health Care*. New York: McGraw-Hill, 2008.

Services provided in a hospital tend to cost more than those provided by clinics. Similarly, doctors cost a lot more than nurses. One way to reduce costs is to provide the same service, with similar health outcomes, in a cheaper place, and performed by a less skilled person. As we show in Chapter 2 on health care, ICTs can help achieve that goal. This is critical in an inequitable world where there will never be enough doctors or hospitals for everyone.

This cost reduction in providing essential services is really key to providing affordable access in tightly resource-constrained environments, as is the ability to provide sophisticated services with less trained people. Pursuing this vision has forced technologists, businesses, academics, leaders, and practitioners alike to think and act more creatively. We have had to move away from our trusted old business models based on wealthy customers' ability to purchase goods and services. Technology must be designed to respect the constraints of the environment and the needs of different groups. When they are ignored, the product or service is doomed to fail.

The fact of the matter is that in this world of limited resources we will never have enough doctors, teachers, or bankers to meet the needs of all people in the world. We have no option but to explore (1) ICT and other innovations targeted at poor populations, (2) new partnerships between the for-profit and not-for-profit entities, and (3) new business models. While it's certainly true that many multinational corporations have found ways to reach poorer consumers—look at fast foods and soft drinks—for-profit businesses cannot, or often will not, solve the challenges of reaching this huge base of potential customers on their own. Innovative partnerships with NGOs, international organizations, and local efforts must all be part of the solution.

That's what this book is all about. Many researched efforts have performed well; some have failed miserably; other ICT methods we have yet to discover may provide positive solutions for many regions. Take, for example, KioskNet.

KIOSKNET TO THE RESCUE[5]

Internet kiosks, or telecenters, provide a great service for people who don't have any other way to send and receive emails and photos or videos—when they work.

Unfortunately, within a few months of installation, all but a few fail. Frustrated users stop coming and, of course, investors become extremely skeptical. Computer kiosks are now empty for several reasons. Weak infrastructure offers intermittent electricity at best, and generators are expensive and require further maintenance. Dial-up often malfunctions in poor rural areas due to floods, landslides, wind-driven misaligned antennas, and faulty construction. Empty kiosks can be partially blamed on unstable software, malfunctioning PCs, and very few available high-cost technicians. No wonder that kiosk companies and collaborating partners become discouraged.

This seems like another good idea rapidly decaying by the wayside. Or is it? Enter KioskNet.

After a conference conversation in 2006, Professor Srinivasan Keshav of Canada's University of Waterloo and his colleagues set out to outfit existing kiosks with cutting-edge wireless technology. KioskNet—a Microsoft-funded three-year research project—now involves more than 20 researchers and various collaborating supporters.

Take some solar panels to recharge the kiosk battery, they suggested. Add a recycled PC, a car battery to power the kiosk during power outages, and a controller box, and—here's the interesting part—pick up the data accumulated in the kiosk server by using a computer mounted in a bus or truck that passes by on a regular basis. The "kiosk ferry" then drives by a "gateway" computer, which is always connected to the Internet, and transfers the kiosk data as well as picks up any data intended for the kiosks along the bus/truck ferry's route. It's a process called "Mechanical Backhaul" and was pioneered by the Massachusetts Institute of Technology's (MIT's) DakNet project for delivering data, but the MIT folks may not have thought of mounting it on an old car or bus. A small rechargeable computer inside the ferry has a WiFi card and storage and a routing protocol.

How about maintenance for outpost kiosk locations often plagued by heat and dust? Kiosk controllers need upgrading and patching from time to time and even semi–field technicians are few and far between. Researchers have devised a threefold backup centralized management and maintenance subsystem that zips and can send updates over one of three channels. It's robust and tolerant and it works.

And here's the best part: The KioskNet project gives away the software to make this work with no patent or copyright restrictions.

Of course, there is still the heat and dust, but creativity knows no bounds and those problems also can be solved by thinking "outside the kiosk," as Keshav and his colleagues have proven.

It's an exciting time to be facing the challenge of feeding, housing, and keeping healthy and safe the four billion and still protect the fragile environment we all call home. There are, however, many difficulties ahead.

WHAT ARE THE BARRIERS TO SUCCESS?

Many once believed that once everyone had access to the Internet, information and communication channels would become universally available. Not true.

Not all e-mail accounts are equal because not all social networks are equal.

—Kentaro Toyama, NetHope Summit,
Redmond, WA, May 20, 2009

They also paid attention only to one-time costs when in reality even low-cost PCs at about $100 per child escalate up to another $250 per year per child when you add in replacement software, breakage, theft, connectivity charges and power, administration expenses, and teacher training.

Many businesses hoping to serve the four billion people at the bottom of the economic pyramid are unaware of the opportunities as well as the problems. For one thing, they have not fostered innovation that meets very different cultural needs. They may have overlooked, for example, that they're designing ICTs for people who can't read or write well and who may be living in an environment where electricity is at best only sporadically available. The businesses may not use appropriate business models since the ability to purchase technology goods is far lower than their usual customers'. They may be unaware of how to price, how to market, how to distribute, and how to nurture a sustainable chain of supply. And they may underestimate how long it will take to enter the market; in other words, they may lack foresight, experience, and patience.

Of course there are many other factors keeping our well-intentioned efforts from succeeding, such as lack of capital, lack of local expertise, cultural differences, suspicion of outside meddling, and the inherent complexity of technology.

WHERE ARE WE TODAY?

Broad awareness of the business potential of the bottom of the pyramid (BoP) exists.[6] Corporations realize that there is a real market for them to serve. More and more companies are realizing that *low* incomes do not mean *no* income. Once people's food and water and other basic needs are met, there is, according to *The Next 4 Billion*, a total base-of-the-pyramid household income of $5 trillion.[7] *That* is the incentive for companies—large and small—to enter those markets.

Targeted Innovation

There is also awareness that new innovation would be required to serve the needs of this market, especially since the ability to enter developing markets in low-income countries using technologies from advanced economies has proven to be a great challenge for technology leaders.

Take the multidisciplinary team approach to research used by Microsoft Research India, formerly headed by Kentaro Toyama, as an example. Many classrooms can afford only one computer, so the team's Multiple Mice for Computers project enables several children to share a single classroom computer for the cost of a few extra mice. They developed software that allows multiple mice with colored cursors to appear on the monitor at the same time. They continue to explore this possibility, and trials reveal that five mice show no visible degradation in the children's ability to interact with the PC. Students become more engaged with software when they are working together. At the same time, they are learning joint decision-making and other collaborative insights and skills. We will soon know if these technologies find success in the marketplace because products have been *commercialized* or made available to customers. In this case, Multiple Mice research has led to real-world products such as Microsoft's MultiPoint Mouse, Mouse Mischief, and the MultiPoint Server in partnership with Hewlett Packard.

In a similarly innovative effort, Microsoft Research India's Digital Green Project, in collaboration with the GREEN Foundation, offers short agricultural videos to marginalized, illiterate farmers with

REAL PRODUCTS CAN MEET REAL DEMANDS

Most governments seek to drive twenty-first century skills for their citizens. Educators want to provide increased student technology access to harness the tools necessary in the global information age. However, most schools cannot afford computers, let alone 1:1 access per student. Recent innovations aim to overcome this challenge through energy-efficient, lower-cost hardware, software, and peripherals.

Shared-resource computing allows one computer's excess capability to support multiple users at the same time, thus lowering acquisition costs, operating expenses, management complexity, and energy consumption. Shared pointers and mice also allow for collaborative learning and increased student–teacher inputs. In this way, products like these can bring the benefits of information technology to the other 90 percent of the world's people.

about three acres of land. The videos focus on sustainable agricultural practices and natural seed diversity. The project maintains a topically indexed online video database for easy downloading and disseminating to a variety of venues available, including "on-street" showings. This kind of training has proven far more effective than any other. This is partly due to the fact that the information contained in the videos is of an immediate and personal nature so that many farmers identify quickly with the videos.

Another research group at the University of California at Berkeley, TIER (Technology and Infrastructure for Emerging

---

INNOVATION FROM EMERGING MARKETS: JOHNSON & JOHNSON'S BABYCENTER

Johnson & Johnson launched its BabyCenter mobile campaign with mobile agency Velti in 2007, first in India and then worldwide. One offshoot targeted young, pregnant Latina women, as PC Internet availability is very poor within this demographic. A *New Media Age* article profiled BabyCenter's global campaign:

> [Pregnant women] were invited to text their due date to a short code to join the community and receive advice and product offers relevant to the stage of the pregnancy.
>
> After 12 months, the community had attracted several thousand members and was achieving retention rates above 90 percent on a monthly repeat opt-in. As a result, BabyCenter rolled out an English version in the United States and now provides the same community-led service, including Booty Caller, a mobile ovulation alert service.
>
> "The powerful aspect of BabyCenter is that it gives new and expectant mums the information they need when they're on the move," says Velti CEO Alex Moukas. "It doesn't try to replicate the website experience on mobile but it does connect with the same community and quality content in an on-the-go experience that can be accessed by all phones. BabyCenter's mobile service can provide constant reassurance and advice a woman can trust."
>
> Steven van Zanen, vice president of product marketing at mobile messaging company Acision, believes the key to the success of the campaign was relevance, which he says underpins all effective examples of mobile marketing: "It was targeted at a very specific audience, and by making it an opt-in service and encouraging users to provide their due dates, Johnson & Johnson could personalize and tailor the campaign to a fine degree."[8]

Regions), is partnering with the National Science Foundation and others such as Intel, Microsoft, and Grameen Bank to create educational tools, such as their locally produced mobile software learning games and programmable cell phones; health-care options; wireless technology (WiLDNet); distributed storage possibilities; and speech technologies. Their low-cost solar-powered WiFi long-distance but locally managed networks now operate in India, Ghana, Guinea-Bissau, and the Philippines. TIER recognizes that because many users are illiterate or semiliterate, spoken language input and output should play a major part in the design of any user interface, which is usually only visual.

These are all examples of innovations that are specifically designed for the needs of the target segments because the existing technologies fall short. But there are other examples where powerful technologies are in search of a business model to reach users in need.

TECHNOLOGY IN SEARCH OF A BUSINESS MODEL[9]

What started as a college class assignment spawned an investigation that could help bring the benefits of modern microscopy to the developing world. Student researchers and their professor at the University of California, Berkeley, have developed a camera-phone microscope powerful enough to diagnose malaria and tuberculosis—diseases that still take a heavy toll in many parts of the world.

While diseases such as malaria and tuberculosis are largely under control in most of the developed world, they remain leading killers in many impoverished countries. Together, the two diseases kill more than 2.5 million people each year—the vast majority in Africa and other developing regions. More than 80 percent of the estimated 881,000 people who died of malaria in 2006 were African children under the age of five, according to the World Health Organization.

(continued)

It was against this grim backdrop that Daniel Fletcher, an associate professor of bioengineering at Berkeley, posed a challenge to students in his optics and microscopy class. Imagine you are working in a remote African village at the time of a disease outbreak, Fletcher told his students, and among your meager supplies you happen to have a camera cell phone and an assortment of basic optics lenses and mounts. Would it be possible to convert the camera phone into a sort of mobile microscope that could be used to diagnose disease? Soon after, Fletcher and his team, with funding from Microsoft Research and others, developed CellScope, powerful enough to use as a microscope in diagnosing tuberculosis and malaria and transmitting images to a physician or medical specialist anywhere in the world.

Overcoming the Barriers of Market-Based Approaches: New Business Models

There is not enough charity or aid to meet the needs of 4 billion people on an ongoing basis. Without sustainable—that is, profitable—businesses involved, efforts to address unmet needs must fall short.

—Allan Hammond, William J. Kramer,
Robert S. Katz, Julia T. Tran, and Courtland Walker,
The Next 4 Billion: Market Size and Business Strategy
at the Base of the Pyramid

Discovering appropriate business models has continued to be a big challenge. Even if technology is available, lack of suitable business models can result in MNCs not entering a market, quitting the market too early, designing the wrong product at the wrong price, and hence risking failure.

Low purchasing power and lack of infrastructure generally mean bigger upfront investment by businesses in developing the manufacturing, distribution, marketing, and sales infrastructure themselves. And it also means lower margins because they have to price their products and services to be affordable. Investments in emerging markets also compete for resources with investments in opportunities in the developed world that offer surer and higher returns.

Companies are experimenting with different pricing, packaging, and distribution models. They are also bringing in innovative financing. These examples have been well documented by Prahalad in his book on the BoP, *The Fortune at the Bottom of the Pyramid.*[10] For example, CEMEX, one of the largest manufacturers of cement in the world, started Patrimonio Hoy in Mexico, a program to allow customers to add onto their homes — one room at a time. Unilever is improving and expanding soap sales, and thus improving health, in remote and rural populations in India by offering smaller-quantity "sachets." There are Indian e-Choupals, information centers linked to the Internet, that connect subsistence farmers with large firms, current agricultural research, and global markets to get better prices for their crops, better yield through better practices, and independence. There are countless other examples of experiments designed to innovate at the margins and many lessons learned.

There is also awareness that MNCs have to play in these markets as a matter of survival because of the disruptive potential of technologies developed to meet the needs of the BoP. There are strategic reasons why MNCs need to care about developing products for this segment because any innovation that addresses those segments will potentially outcompete MNCs' offerings in the developed markets. We can already see this happening in the telecommunications market. Network operators in India and China have innovated in their business models to where they can be profitable while having the lowest and most affordable rates. Now their ambitions are becoming global and they are beginning to compete with European and U.S. operators. Similar stories can be told in other industries as well, such as Suzlon in wind energy, Mahindra in tractors, and Huawei in telecommunications gear. There is even a name for this phenomenon: *reverse innovation.* Companies like GE have taken this to heart and are using this strategy to develop medical devices. They are, however, the exception.[11]

Unconventional Partnerships, Unconventional Business Models

Just as businesses are reorganizing around the need to open up to innovative partnerships with NGOs and the public sector to benefit the impoverished, and doing so through a sustainable business model, in parallel the nonprofit world is realizing that sustainability of many development initiatives is hard to achieve without a viable business model. By combining their efforts, many organizations and businesses have made outstanding progress in addressing these emerging markets by better understanding product design and the real needs that exist.

We are seeing a new breed of *public–private partnerships*—those involving corporations, governments, universities, and intergovernmental agencies like the United Nations, World Bank, and NGOs. In fact, a new breed of organization is gaining currency—*social enterprises*—which are both business-savvy and results oriented. In our view, they are undervalued by for-profit firms seeking to enter developing world markets. These social enterprises are leading the way in adapting traditional business models to emerging markets and in meeting the world's most pressing needs through business and community practice.

Social enterprises consider the context of impoverished regions and have built successful business models that the for-profit sector can replicate, partner with, or expand upon. As businesses that seek to make the world a better place through their entrepreneurial focus on the common good, they are able to offer unique solutions to the world's problems that have emerged from local communities in need. Social ventures view the private sector far differently than those that consider MNCs as merely exploitative, instead viewing the private sector as a technology enabler locally, regionally, and globally. Since government programs are limited and donor funding intermittent, the private sector also offers a chance for long-term sustainability.

> *We bring an entrepreneurial attitude to our social mission, and we are committed to working with—instead of against—governments and the private sector.*
>
> *—Bridges.org*

Within poorer nations, governments and NGOs have played a prominent role in social and economic development. Both sectors have traditionally been slow to adopt technologies. The latter, however, has proven more effective than both the public and private sectors in identifying and securing new market opportunities, especially where none existed before.[12]

PEDAL PUMPS AND MORE[13]

In India, 70 percent of the farming population cultivates tiny farms that grow even smaller each year because of rapid population growth. Farms are rain-fed and monsoon driven, with few alternative sources of irrigation. Large farmers can afford diesel-operated water pumps. An Indian not-for-profit organization, IDEI (International Development Enterprises of India), saw the need to engage in the development of simple and affordable pedal pumps for small farm and other relevant technologies for farming and water irrigation. Thanks to donor funds, IDEI is now active in ten Indian states. Since its inception in 1991, 350,000 farmers in northeastern India alone, where water tables are high, have purchased pedal or treadle pumps.

In more arid parts of India, IDEI supplies AdITI kits—affordable drip-irrigation technologies enabling growers to produce off-season crops—to 85,000 small or marginal farmers. Women, in particular, are benefiting from this micro-irrigation technology that delivers water

(continued)

directly to the roots of plants. They are now able to stay at home to operate the light bucket-and-drum kits, providing needed income they otherwise had to get by traveling to often-exploitive mills and factories. They no longer fear harassment, nor do they have to leave their young children with older siblings. Furthermore, their farm-fresh vegetable and fruit diets have shown a remarkable increase in healthier families.

Because isolated interventions are rarely sustainable, IDEI partners with various stakeholders to create a strong demand for the technology along with a dependable supply chain: NGOs, market forces, and agriculture and research institutions work along with the farmers to create more stable production and markets. This synergy stimulates the private sector to provide affordably priced tools and technologies and at the same time creates a pro-poor market raising the level of small farm incomes.

Another IDEI project focuses on removing obstacles to both buyer and seller in the marketplace, along with training farmers in successful crop management and output marketing.

At the time of this writing, IDEI has a viable network of about 35 manufacturers, 100 distributors, 325 dealers, 1620 assemblers, and 225 NGOs to support the output keeping 450,000 farmers in business. That's a lot of pedal pumps—and more!

These business models take significant time and experimentation to develop (often five years or more). This creates a significant problem for the investment time horizons of for-profit organizations seeking to tap the bottom of the pyramid as quickly as possible. NGOs are able to do much more of the initial creation of the business model infrastructure. This suggests a surefire formula to resolve the time–horizon issue for for-profit companies: Engage with NGOs to assist in the discovery and creation of business models. From the NGOs' perspective, enlisting the involvement of for-profit firms creates sustainability for a technology and scaling up of the impact, and enables the social enterprise to exit and search out the next opportunity.

KICKSTART: A SUCCESSFUL BUSINESS MODEL

Hoping to eradicate poverty by building a middle class from the bottom up, Nick Moon and Martin Fisher started ApproTEC in 1991 in Nairobi, Kenya. In 2005, Approtec became KickStart. According to KickStart's website, "their model was based on a five-step process to develop, launch and promote simple money-making tools that poor entrepreneurs could use to create their own profitable businesses."[14] KickStart designs and develops low-cost tools, equipment, manuals, and business plans required for establishing small enterprises in Kenya and Tanzania and Mali, among the world's poorest nations. There is much to be learned from the firm's comprehensive approach. Its most successful product, thus far, is its Super MoneyMaker (SMM) manually operated irrigation pump. *Fast Company* pointed out in 2005:

> East African farmers who buy the SMM irrigation pump easily recoup their investment in their first crop cycle and, in Kenya, are making more than $1,100 profit per year, increasing their annual farm income by a factor of 10 and more than doubling their total income. For the first time they can properly feed and educate their families, pay for health-care, and invest in their futures. They are on an upward spiral of growth rather than a downward spiral of poverty.[15]

But more than creating usable products, the company makes an effort to build and develop the entire value network for its product in a market where the nodes of the network—manufacturers, distributors, finance providers, marketing partners, and others—are not initially present and functioning at a level necessary for the success of the business model. KickStart takes a leadership role at all levels of the network with the goal of eventually allowing each node to achieve sustainable profitability. As a result, the risk is reduced for the entrepreneur and coordination is built into the entire business system.

KickStart has its own commissioned sales staff and promotes the new technologies and installs them in the private sector to ensure that they are well known, easily available, and purchased by thousands of small-scale investors. The firm recruits and trains a

(continued)

network of local retail shops and then buys the technologies from the manufacturers and sells them with a markup to the retailers. Finally, the company develops cost-effective marketing tools to promote and market the new equipment to local entrepreneurs, including:

- Live demonstrations at the retailers
- Radio and newspaper advertisements
- Mobile truck-mounted demonstrations in local villages
- Demonstrations at local shows and exhibitions

The local entrepreneurs/investors buy the technologies from the retailers and use them to establish profitable new businesses. By reducing investment and risk, and increasing coordination, KickStart increases the chance that these entrepreneurs will be profitable, promoting sustainability for the business. Note, though, that KickStart does not attempt to eliminate risk from the distribution channel. Entrepreneurs must still make risky investments and compete with others for the business. This imposes market discipline on the distribution system.

It measures the number of new businesses and jobs created and the amount of new profits and new wages earned by the new entrepreneurs and their employees. These impacts are compared to the costs of the program. This enables KickStart to learn from its experience, and develop best practices for future initiatives.[16]

Before a new product is introduced, KickStart makes sure they have the market research identifying small business opportunities. Then the firm designs a low-cost tool or piece of equipment, develops a sustainable and profitable supply chain from manufacturer to retailer, and then mass-markets that new technology to the farmers or other rural residents. Once the company's critical mass of buyers has been reached, it no longer markets the product. At that point, sales will continue to grow without more promotion.

By June of 2010, this business model has led to the following impressive results:

- 150,000 pumps have been sold
- 97, 500 new businesses have been started.
- 288,000 people have moved out of poverty with annual profits and wages in excess of $98 million dollars[17]

There are many similarities between a master franchisor in a developed economy and a social enterprise. They both must develop the entire business architecture, and recruit outsiders to invest their own time and money in a portion of that architecture in order to bring it into being.[18] During the initial bootstrapping of the value network, the nonprofits are the hubs of that network. Unlike master franchisors in advanced economies, though, the social enterprise leaves the great majority of profits for local small businesses in order to build a sustainable economic ecosystem and provide incentives for local entrepreneurs. The creation of profits throughout the value chain is critical for NGOs and social enterprises to be able to move on and allow local small businesses to sustain the manufacturing, sales, and installation of the products. Nonprofits may better address developing-world issues because of their long time horizons, their alignment with the community interest, and their comprehension of the overall context of use. Nonprofits primarily focus on social benefits, and see the profit model as a means to that end. Nonprofits view the profit model as an exit option that facilitates sustainability once the nonprofits have moved on to new initiatives.

Success Strategies

Allen Hammond and his colleagues, who created *The Next 4 Billion*, outline four broad critical strategies for success:

> 1. Focusing on the BOP with unique products, unique services, or unique technologies that are appropriate to BOP needs and that require completely reimagining the business, often through significant investment of money and management talent. Examples are found in such sectors as water (point-of-use systems), food (healthier products), finance (microfinance and low-cost remittance systems), housing, and energy.
> 2. Localizing value creation through franchising, through agent strategies that involve building local ecosystems of vendors or suppliers, or by treating the community as the customer, all of which usually involve substantial investment in capacity building and training. Examples can be seen in health care

(franchise and agent-based direct marketing), ICT (local phone entrepreneurs and resellers), food (agent-based distribution systems), water (community-based treatment systems), and energy (mini-hydropower systems).

3. Enabling access to goods or services . . . [This may involve different packaging strategies that lower purchase barriers, prepaid or other innovative business models that achieve the same result, or the use of alternative financing and distribution strategies or deployment of low-cost technologies.] Examples occur in food, ICT, and consumer products (in packaging goods and services in small unit sizes, or "sachets") and in health care (such as cross-subsidies and community-based health insurance). And cutting across many sectors are financing strategies that range from microloans to mortgages.

4. Unconventional partnering with governments, NGOs, or groups of multiple stakeholders to bring the necessary capabilities to the table. Examples are found in energy, transportation, health care, financial services, and food and consumer goods.[19]

Based on successful deployments, we conclude that the successful innovative products have been implemented through a business model that was locally relevant and customized. And sound leadership and assistance to local entrepreneurs were provided in order to build up sustainable networks that can continue to deliver the product into the marketplace.

Introducing technology to the poor, for instance, has been attempted in various forms. One of the more successful methods is the Grameen Bank's "phone ladies," who live in areas without phone services. Dr. Muhammad Yunus founded a bank in Bangladesh ready to provide loans of about $100. Bangladesh alone now has 7 million borrowers, 95 percent of whom are women, since men are more likely to be credit risks while women generally pay back the loans. Hajera Begum is one phone lady who bought her "business in a box"—a Finnish-made mobile phone, a battery charger, a stopwatch, a calculator, and an advertising signboard—to set up her business for about $400; she makes weekly payback installments of $5. She charges her neighborhood

MICROSOFT ADDRESSES NEEDS, CONFRONTS BARRIERS, AND REALIZES MARKET POTENTIAL[20]

Microsoft has made a long-term commitment to research and development on (and increasingly *in*) emerging markets and innovative partnerships required to reach new and potential clients.

Raising Awareness

Microsoft Research ran multiple requests for proposals (RFPs) to identify and fund research in universities around the world to advance the state-of-the-art technologies relevant to challenges of the developing world. Some of these have been global and some have focused on regions such as India and Latin America. They have targeted advances in technology for applications in education, health, environment, and microeconomics. Some examples of the problems tackled are:

- Create new infrastructures, form factors, and applications of mobile devices (which include mobile phones or embedded devices).
- Improve connectivity, particularly in environments without existing network infrastructures or with intermittent availability, to networking and power. Challenges in wireless networks would be a relevant theme in this category.
- Design appropriate user interfaces addressing challenges in literacy and for novice users of technology.

While the initial funding was around $3 million, Microsoft was the first company of its size and scale to legitimize this field of research. One aspect of the RFPs that was unique was that this was a partnership between corporate research and community affairs and encouraged academics to partner with NGOs to submit and implement their proposals. Now, many more agencies have an active program to pursue these areas of inquiry and many have matched their own funding to push the research further.

(continued)

Microsoft has also created competitions such as the Imagine Cup and Developers Without Borders to encourage nascent developer communities to create innovative technologies. Imagine Cup, Microsoft's annual technology development competition for students from around the world, challenges participants to create software solutions that address a specific societal need, ranging from education to health care to the environment.[21]

To give the community a forum and voice to publish and discuss research in this space, Microsoft became a founding member of the IEEE/ACM International Conference on Information and Communication Technologies and Development (ICTD). Former Microsoft chairman Bill Gates served as its keynote speaker in 2009 in Doha Qatar, and the journal (*ITID*) that was spun out of the first ICTD conference event is already considered a top venue for publishing in this field. On the ground, its Community Affairs teams have been working globally in over 110 countries in support of expanding access to community-centered technology centers. The program has a digital literacy curriculum, and sponsors community technology centers that often serve as training centers for the local population. The group also has a program in NGO capacity building through TechSoup and Telecentre.org nonprofit programs. The company has also co-funded the *ITID* journal for the past several years, providing the opportunity for academics to publish peer-reviewed works.

Conducting Research

Microsoft's Bangalore lab, which opened in January 2005, represents the company's effort to tap into India's rich university research community and considerable software engineering talent. The Technology for Emerging Markets research group has been a pioneer in applying both social-science research and technology innovation toward the needs and aspirations of two kinds of communities worldwide: emerging markets, whose members are increasingly able to afford computing technologies and services, and underserved communities, for whom access to computing remains largely out of reach. This multidisciplinary group has been responsible for work on microfinance, social entrepreneurship, intra-family technology sharing, and children's sharing of resources. In addition to influential work on text-free interfaces, the group's work on multiple mice for shared computing has been expanded and made available to emerging-market users. The group also contributes to worldwide efforts in information and communication technology for development and to Microsoft's Unlimited Potential efforts in emerging markets.

Creating New Business Models

One of the company's goals is to provide the most appropriate applications and technologies for new markets and the platforms that local content developers can fully utilize. Business groups have developed new models and products to service low- and middle-income segments of the world. Through shared-access devices, prepaid/postpaid solutions, mobile plays such as health-care applications with CARE and microfinance tool with FINCA, it enables access and tailored services to its new customers in the majority of the world. With lower-cost pricing models for software in some countries, Microsoft is working to enable an infrastructure and platforms that broaden its base of users to learn, to communicate, and to share.

villagers a nominal fee to send and receive calls from her phone. Grameen and their international partners who own and operate the phone system bill her about 4 cents a minute for outgoing calls and a dollar a minute for international calls. Incoming calls are not billed. Phone ladies have now formed a national network and are the basis for an expanding high-tech industry. They earn about three times as much as the average annual income. Village phone projects are currently underway in Uganda, Rwanda, Indonesia, Cambodia, the Philippines, and Haiti.

In a similar vein, solar energy systems designed by Grameen are being rented out by their owners so they can augment their incomes and break out of poverty.

Success Stories

We will be highlighting many of these global success stories, some market based, some representing unique innovations, in the pages that follow. Here are some quick snapshots of a few of them:

- Research labs and universities such as Microsoft Research; University of California, Berkeley; Carnegie Mellon; and Massachusetts Institute of Technology have successfully grappled with access gaps using cell phones, low-cost wireless, and other technologies.
- A team of researchers at the Massachusetts Institute of Technology worked to create wireless sensor networks to provide early flood detection in underserved countries.
- A team of researchers at the University of Buenos Aires is developing technologies to marry wireless smartphones to low-cost diagnostic tools such as electrocardiograms to send preventive care information.
- The Intel-powered Classmate PC, a rugged laptop for kids, with its lightweight design and water-resistant keyboard, is looking promising for low-income classroom use.
- In March 2007, Kenya's largest mobile network operator, Safaricom (part of the Vodafone Group), launched M-Pesa, an innovative payment service for the unbanked. Its rapid take-up is a clear sign that there is market demand for faster, cheaper, and more efficient ways of moving money.
- Celtel, an entrepreneurial company operating in some of the poorest and least stable countries in Africa, went from start-up to telecom giant in just seven years.

Action Plan

The most critical step for an MNC planning to venture into this space is to understand the problem that has to be solved and to determine whether technology and business models exist to help solve it.

As Figure 1.2 illustrates, if the technology doesn't exist, then you have to go back to R&D to help create it, from ground zero

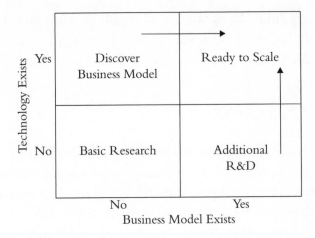

Figure 1.2 Action Plan

or by modifying existing technologies. If, however, the technology exists, but the business model is not clear, this has to be discovered. This process can be long and expensive, because the margins are small due to the limited purchasing power of the target segment, and significant returns can take a long time to materialize. As we pointed out earlier through many examples, NGOs can help at this stage due to the way they operate and their nonprofit motive. They also have the local context and relationships that can reduce the cost of discovery. Hence the optimal strategy in this case is to partner with NGOs to discover the business model and build local capacity.

If both the business model and the technology are known and tested, the real impact comes from scaling up. MNCs have the means and knowledge to do that. Through the scaling up, they not only become sustainable as a business; they can impact a larger number of people in a positive way. Since this is closer to their core strength, they can rely on their more conventional partnerships.

The most expensive mistakes happen when the MNCs do not accurately identify the nature of the problem and the maturity of the technology and business models available to solve it. If the technology doesn't work, business models can't sustain it and any entry is premature. If the business models don't work, the companies will likely lose a lot of money before deciding to exit. They are also less likely to reconsider the opportunity later.

SUMMARY POINTS

- ICT has the potential to positively impact the lives of those at the bottom of the pyramid by providing products and services in a resource- and skill-constrained environment.
- Successfully meeting these needs requires targeted innovation, appropriate business models, and partnerships between the for-profit and the not-for-profit world.
- Products and services have to be designed to meet the local context and must be affordable, relevant, and accessible.
- Enough evidence is emerging about what works and what doesn't in the fields of health, education, environment, and finance to guide the MNCs. The pipeline of innovations is also becoming richer.
- The action plan for MNCs requires them to determine the nature of the needs and the availability of appropriate technology or business models, and then develop local partnerships to meet those needs.
- If MNCs do not develop products and services specifically targeted for the emerging economies, they are likely to get disrupted by local companies that perfect a business model that is profitable with low margins. These companies will eventually compete with MNCs in their local strongholds.

NOTES

1. Rabin Patra, Joyojeet Pal, Sergiu Nedevschi, Madelaine Plauche, and Udai Pawar "Usage Models of Classroom Computing in Developing Regions," Second International Conference on Information Technologies and Development, IEEE Conference Proceedings, Bangalore, December 2007.

2. Allen L. Hammond, William J. Kramer, Robert S. Katz, Julia T. Tran, and Courtland Walker, *The Next 4 Billion: Market Size and Business Strategy at the Base of the Pyramid* (World Resources Institute and International Finance Corporation / World Bank Group, 2007).

3. C. K. Prahalad and Allen Hammond, "Serving the World's Poor, Profitably," *Harvard Business Review*, 80(9): 48–58, 2002.

4. Clayton Christensen, Jerome H. Grossman, and Jason Hwang, *The Innovator's Prescription: A Disruptive Solution for Health Care* (New York: McGraw-Hill, 2008).

5. Srinivasan Keshav, "The KioskNet Project," http://blizzard.cs.uwaterloo.ca/tetherless/index.php/KioskNet (accessed July 14, 2010).

6. C. K. Prahalad and Stuart L. Hart, "The Fortune at the Bottom of the Pyramid," *strategy + business*, Issue 26, September 2002; C. K. Prahalad, *The Fortune at the Bottom of the Pyramid: Eradicating Poverty through Profits* (Philadelphia: Wharton School Publishing, 2006); and Stuart L. Hart, *Capitalism at the Crossroads* (Philadelphia: Wharton School Publishing, 2005).

7. Hammond, Kramer, Katz, Tran, and Walker, *The Next 4 Billion: Market Size and Business Strategy at the Base of the Pyramid.*

8. David Murphy, "NMA Global Campaigns," *New Media Age*, www.nma.co.uk/features/global-campaigns/3003382.article, August 13, 2009.

9. Microsoft Research, "CellScope Could Offer Low-Cost Portable Options for Disease Diagnosis," http://research.microsoft.com/en-us/collaboration/focus/health/cellscope.pdf, 2008.

10. Prahalad, *The Fortune at the Bottom of the Pyramid.*

11. Jeffrey R. Immelt, Vijay Govindarajan, and Chris Trimble, "How GE Is Disrupting Itself," *Harvard Business Review*, October 2009.

12. Henry W. Chesbrough, Shane Ahern, Megan Finn, and Stephane Guerraz. "Business Models for Technology in the Developing World: The Role of Non-Governmental Organizations." *California Management Review* 338 (May 1, 2006).

13. International Development Enterprises (India): www.ide-india.org/ide/index1.shtml (accessed July 14, 2010).

14. KickStart, "About KickStart," www.kickstart.org/about-us (accessed July 26, 2010).

15. "ApproTEC: Winner's Statement," *Fast Company*, www.fastcompany.com/social/2005/statements/approtec.html (accessed July 14, 2010).

16. Chesbrough, Ahern, Finn, and Guerraz, "Business Models for Technology in the Developing World."

17. Martin Fisher, "Income Is Development: KickStart's Pumps Help Kenyan Farmers Transition to a Cash Economy," *Innovations* 1(1), Winter 2006.

18. Chesbrough, Ahern, Finn, and Guerraz, "Business Models for Technology in the Developing World."

19. Hammond, Kramer, Katz, Tran, and Walker, *The Next 4 Billion: Market Size and Business Strategy at the Base of the Pyramid.*

20. Microsoft, "Unlimited Potential," www.microsoft.com/about/corporatecitizenship/en-us/about/unlimited-potential (accessed July 26, 2010).

21. Microsoft, "Imagine Us," www.imagineusgulf.com (accessed March 2, 2010).

CHAPTER 2

HEALTH CARE

WHERE AND WHEN IT IS NEEDED

WORLD HEALTH

One of the most effective interventions in public health, after the invention of toilets, chlorination of drinking water, addition of iodine in salt, childhood vaccinations, and such, has to have been the "barefoot doctor" experiment by the Chinese after the revolution.[1] Since there were not enough trained doctors or nurses in China, the government trained a large cadre of regular folks in the basics of hygiene and diagnosis and treatment of common conditions. They sent them out to all parts of the country, ensuring that even the remotest village had access to such a practitioner. The result was a dramatic improvement in public health and a reduction of infant mortality and increase in longevity.

The experiment did not survive, however, due to its dependence on government subsidies; the lack of continuing education, which made the practitioner's knowledge obsolete; and the privatization of medicine that followed after China opened up to the world. But the problems that the Chinese set out to address still exist today—except on a larger, worldwide scale. In response, a new model of trained health-care workers is emerging, except unlike those who preceded them, these workers are now equipped with sophisticated phones, medical sensors, and applications, and connected to the best experts and the resources of the Internet. And they can bring health care to regions of the world where none existed and to people who could not afford it before.

Health is not merely the absence of disease or infirmity. The World Health Organization defines health as a state of complete physical, mental, and social well-being. Four billion people currently live in places where a state of good health is merely a dream, and about one billion of them are so poor that their lives are truly at risk. As Jeffrey Sachs, economist and poverty writer, once put it: "They are just too poor to stay alive."[2]

A shortage of doctors and nurses, ill-equipped or nonexistent hospitals and clinics, and expensive medications are only a few of the challenges faced by people at the bottom of the economic pyramid. Often without the protection of their government or private insurance, they resort to less optimum choices ranging from self-diagnosis to delayed treatment, or worse. In Burundi, for example, Human Rights Watch reports that even government hospitals routinely detain patients who are unable to pay or even sequester them for months in abysmal conditions. When people are sick, whole societies lose and diseases threaten entire populations.

Despite their poverty, households at this lowest level of the world's economic pyramid actually do spend $150 billion a year on health goods and services, according to *The Next 4 Billion*.[3] Researchers and designers are just now beginning to address *affordable, accessible* and *relevant* health information technologies to meet their demand.

We already have established that the poor can and will pay for their own care, if it is reasonably priced. Nothing is more valuable to people than healthcare, and by paying, they feel less like beggars and more like "customers" who can and should demand quality care.
—Muhammad Yunus, Huffington Post, April 2009

What Does Affordable Mean?

In the recent past, *affordable* might have meant offering a $500,000 medical imaging machine for $50,000. But now we can offer a $5,000 portable mobile phone–based medical imaging system through targeted research and development.

The Grameen Eye Care Hospital in Bangladesh and the Aravind Hospital can now do cataract surgery for $25, thanks in large part to the efficiency brought about by their use of information and communication technologies (ICTs). And when it comes to the delivery of babies, incubators that often cost upward of $20,000 can now be found for as low as $25, along with essential diagnostic instruments that are tough, cheap, and reusable. One affordable goal for doctor-attended births is $40 — that's less than one-fourth of the cost in traditional hospitals.

Accessible Care—A Major Consideration

A large piece of health care depends on how we manage information and make it accessible to health-care professionals in real time. For instance, ClickHealth, a health ecosystem (www.clickhealth .org), provides access to medical specialists in underserved areas and collects real-time data for interventions. This mobile-based telemedicine service is built around microcredit for health workers and micro–health insurance for patients, making it accessible and affordable. It offers remote diagnostics and health-risk assessment and early warning systems and started testing HIV/AIDS staging and cervical cancer diagnostics protocols in Botswana in 2009. It also offers mobile phone software and inexpensive tools for local health-care agents, a web-based interface for remote specialists, back-end systems for data routing, a viable network of "remote" medical specialists, health-worker training, and monitoring and supervision for quality control. Our own government in the United States is now funding better electronic health record keeping.

What's Relevant Today, and What Will Be Relevant in the Future?

Listening to local people state their needs leads to relevant care. Basing decisions on what underserved areas need on what Western medicine offers may lead to disappointment and financial losses.

> *By 2015, a large number of the world's poor will live in poor, remote areas of what will by then be middle-income countries. For these countries, the problem will not be a question of sufficient resources for healthcare but of how those resources are being distributed.*
> *—Jacques van der Gaag, International Food Policy Research Institute*

Health-care delivery depends on access to relevant, reliable knowledge in forms that are appropriate, readily assimilated, and easily applied, whether fulfilled by a biomedical researcher, a nurse, a doctor, a midwifery student, or a mother. Caregivers depend on quality information and actionable knowledge for their patients and this makes modern IT a critical element of health infrastructure— not a luxury that benefits a few.

The World Bank claims that by 2015, the major killers of today—communicable diseases such as malaria, tuberculosis, and AIDS—will be replaced by cancer, diabetes, obesity, and heart disease—the chronic illnesses prevalent in wealthier countries. How can ICT help in the preventive medical area? Curbing tobacco use and reducing obesity, high cholesterol, and high blood pressure outside the clinical settings will be valid options, of course, as they are in the United States today. Providing *relevant and timely health-care information* will become more important than ever for low-income countries.

> *The most common mistake among unsuccessful market-based solutions is to confuse what low-income customers or suppliers ostensibly need with what they actually want. Many enterprises have pushed offer-ings into the market only to see them fail. People living at the*

base of the economic pyramid should be seen as customers and not beneficiaries; they will spend money, or switch livelihoods, or invest valuable time, only if they calculate the transaction will be worth their while.

—Ashish Karamchandani, Michael Kubzansky, and Paul Frandano, "Emerging Markets, Emerging Models"

It is also critical to come up with low-cost diagnosis and treatment options suitable for people with the lowest disposable incomes in the world. But beyond treatment and diagnostic technologies, there is a significant need to bridge the knowledge and information gap faced by developing world health-care systems and providers. And contrary to popular belief that they are a luxury, information and communication technologies play a critical role across the entire health-care ecosystem, because a large piece of health care *is* the information management problem. This system involves complex interactions between patients, medical practitioners, funding organizations, regulatory bodies, information systems, and research providers within specific cultural contexts—all of which rely on information and knowledge to be effective.

Changing the Economics

As we show in Figure 2.1, costs of health-care services provided are largely determined by where those services are provided and by the skill level of the person providing those services. Services provided in a hospital tend to cost more than those provided at clinics. Similarly, doctors cost a lot more than nurses. One way to reduce costs is to provide the same services, with similar health outcomes, in a cheaper place, and performed by a less skilled person. In this chapter, we explore how ICT is reducing the costs and/or the level of skill required for delivering health-care services in the following critical areas:

- Health education
- Health administration and management

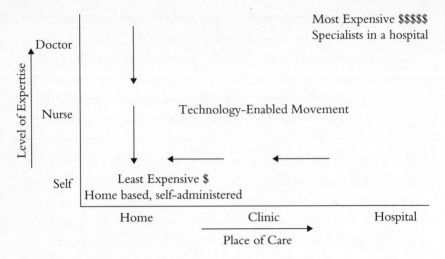

Figure 2.1 Impact of ICT on Health Care

Source: Adapted from Clayton Christensen, Jerome H. Grossman, and Jason Hwang, *The Innovator's Prescription: A Disruptive Solution for Health Care.* New York: McGraw-Hill, 2008.

- Telemedicine
- Diagnosis and prevention
- Disease surveillance and information gathering

Myths Surrounding Health Care

Prevailing myths about health care and treatment have to be demystified to allow IT to better assist in increasing affordable access for more people. Some myths claim:

- **You can have a one-stop shop.** You can't, because no two patients are alike. Health, by definition, is highly individual and depends on local contexts. Today's multiple methods of health care demand a supportive network and local, individualized solutions.
- **IT is a luxury only wealthy health-care providers and patients can afford.** Health care is part of a system and

systems need to communicate with one another. IT is no longer a luxury, but a necessity—for everyone.

- **Solutions to health-care problems should be handled by local professionals.** Unconventional partnerships (between individuals, academic and corporate researchers, multinational corporations, government, international organizations, nongovernmental organizations [NGOs], etc.) can provide ongoing sustainable health solutions. Local knowledge often needs to be complemented with external, specialized expertise.

- **The best way to educate the public is through radio, television, and interactive websites.** In addition to radio, in the developing world, short messaging service (SMS) messages are proving to be most effective for HIV/AIDS. SMS respects people's privacy and gives them the tools they need to make informed choices.

HEALTH EDUCATION

Providing professional health education is critical in two distinct ways. First, continuing education for medical staff is needed, as well as semiskilled training for paraprofessionals. Second, education enables people to increase control over their own health and improve their quality of life.

As we see in the next two case study examples, ICT can help people bypass the traditional and logistical barriers to education by reducing time, compressing distance, and working through and around the local infrastructure.

Professional health education comes in many forms. It may be formal training at a credible institution or it may be just-in-time learning. For established health caregivers, it may be timely health information. It's safe to say that no matter where we live, we all need more access to good health information, information that's

PROJECT MASILULEKE: "FOR HOPE AND WARM COUNSEL, PCM [PLEASE CALL ME]"[4]

By some estimates, 40 percent of South Africans are infected with HIV/AIDS, yet only 2 percent have ever been tested. Only one out of ten people identified with the disease are being treated. That sad fact means 90 percent will die.

Beginning in 2009, mobile technology together with a coalition of partners (iTeach, the Praekelt Foundation, Nokia Siemens Networks, and the National Geographic Society, to name just a few) now brings hope, as the name *Masiluleke* means. This "warm counsel" comes privately, honoring the cultural stigma this disease imposes.

About a million messages are broadcast across the continent of Africa each day over the free "Please Call Me" SMS unused message space (120 spare characters). A typical message connecting users to trained operators at HIV and TB call centers might look like this:

Text Message
From gustavpraek
Please call me: 0824245716
HIV + being mistreated by your
family or friends? For
confidential counseling call
AIDS helpline on 0800012342

The operators on the other end of the call provide accurate health-care information and counseling and refer people to local testing clinics. Text messages will also remind people of their clinic visits and to take their drugs.

The next phase of the Masiluleke plan is to install "virtual call centers," where existing helplines will incorporate "gold star" knowledgeable HIV patients who are trained to speak to other patients. This will not only extend effective care, but create hundreds of additional health-care-provider jobs.

SPREAD THE MESSAGE, STOP THE VIRUS[5]

A similar nonprofit program is called "Text to Change." Nine partners have joined together to address Millennium Development Goal 6 (halting the spread of HIV/AIDS and rolling back HIV infections by 2015). They also use SMS message campaigns to provide HIV/AIDS education primarily in Uganda and develop their own software and hardware. Their pioneer quiz message, "Don't guess the answers. Learn the Truth about AIDS" has to date gotten close to an 18 percent response rate. They plan to use text messaging to create a dialogue about HIV/AIDS, to reduce its stigma and discrimination, and to motivate people to be tested and treated.

usable and relevant to practices. Poor information, however, can actually be detrimental, according to Tessa Tan-Torres Edejer, creating a "negative feedback loop."[6]

"South to South Science" is a global effort by nations that traditionally have looked to Western medical solutions (which often failed) but now have a clearer vision of what they are able to provide for themselves. They now see themselves as active generators of solutions rather than passive recipients. But to offer solutions more effectively, information must be effectively disseminated.

Countries are combining research programs on AIDS, malaria, and other diseases whose impact is most heavily felt in the developing world creating joint protocols for independently assessing the safety of genetically modified crops; dramatically ramping up basic science education; setting up scientific educational exchanges; signing agreements to increase research funding; and hosting conferences on the scientific priorities of developing nations versus those of the developed world.

—Alex Steffen, Bruce Sterling, and Al Gore,
Worldchanging

HEALTHLINE GOES TO PAKISTAN WITH SPEECH-BASED TELEPHONE INFORMATION[7]

Community health workers (CHWs), usually women, are now receiving training in how to provide basic health care and to determine how severely ill their patients are. Their effectiveness depends on how they are trained, keeping in mind that many cannot read.

Realizing they must be trained and supported without written language, a team of Carnegie Mellon University researchers stepped up. Led by Dr. Roni Rosenfeld, Dr. Rahul Tongia, and Jahanzeb Sherwani, they created a speech-based toll-free medical information system. Speech recognition systems had previously been used mainly for booking tickets or getting travel information, but very little was known about the design principles for medical information—or any number of other purposes for people in the developing world.

> The benefit of our system is that you don't need a smartphone, you don't need a desktop computer, you don't need a laptop—you just need someone that can make a phone call.
>
> —Jahanzeb Sherwani

Most CHWs visit patients in their homes and most homes do not have landlines. Therefore, Healthline was designed to be accessible by cell phones as well as landline phones. Partnership provides positive results, once again. The Aga Khan University in Karachi, Pakistan, provided the technical leadership, and the Health and Nutrition Development Society provided the services and the funding for the initiative. The first phase of this research offered recorded information in Urdu about diarrhea and pneumonia. If the user mentioned the word "pneumonia," for instance, the system would offer seven subtopics, including prevention and treatment. Vocally, the user could at any time have the information repeated or go to another topic. Researchers learned that they needed to adapt the language from health pamphlets, for instance, to the more auditory-friendly context. Information is being expanded to include information on many more health topics, including diabetes, hepatitis, and sexually transmitted diseases. Eventually, the researchers hope, the speech model will be used throughout Pakistan as well as in other countries.

The Microsoft Research Digital Inclusion Program provided $1.2 million in research funding for 17 recipients from 34 countries, and the Carnegie Mellon Healthline project was one of them. The success of Healthline, as with all new technology, is dependent on cross-education with people in the field.

Those of us who develop the technology and know what it can do don't always know what it can be good for. People in the field sometimes underestimate or overestimate what technology can do. The process of cross-education is very bandwidth intensive. We hit upon people who right away bought into the idea and got excited about it. They understood it. If we can make it work decently, they will come.

—Roni Rosenfeld, Professor, Carnegie Mellon University

Providing access to reliable health information for health workers in developing countries is potentially the single most cost effective and achievable strategy for sustainable improvement in healthcare.
—N. Pakenham-Walsh, British Medical Journal

In Kenya, only 15 percent of the 20,000 nurses have sufficient training to treat major diseases such as HIV/AIDS, tuberculosis, and malaria. Therefore, AMREF (African Medical and Research Foundation) has partnered with the Kenyatta National Hospital to create an e-learning model with the goal of registering 20,000 more nurses by 2011.[8] The Virtual Nursing School in Nairobi has set up 100 e-learning centers all across Kenya and 27 other nursing schools have implemented the program.[9] By 2008, more than 2,000 nurses were enrolled. The program helps health workers upgrade from being enrolled nurses to being registered community health nurses. They work as they learn.

This is not just collaboration on training, but a demonstration of how private—public partnerships should work. As AMREF builds Kenyatta's capacity for training, the hospital will become a resource centre for other hospitals to train nurses and other health workers in a similar manner across the country.
—Dr. Muli-Musiime, deputy director of AMREF

Research tells us that the less income people have, the more likely they are to yield to unhealthy behaviors to take the edge off their hardship.

> *Tobacco, after all, is an antidepressant, alcohol is a sedative, and comfort foods dampen the release of stress hormones in the body, as well as increase the production of dopamine—a brain chemical that produces feelings of pleasure. . . . Accordingly, research documents that the less income people have, the more likely they are to smoke, binge drink, and eat a sugary, fatty diet. These behavioral patterns are reflected in people's spending patterns: poor people spend a larger portion of their incomes on alcohol and tobacco than do more affluent people.*
> —*Aneel Karnani*, Stanford Social Innovation Review

ICT can offer widespread dissemination of public service health messages aimed at changing behavior for healthier living. Besides continuing education of health workers, ICT allows open access to medical knowledge, anywhere in the world.

HEALTH ADMINISTRATION AND MANAGEMENT

Health-care systems vary considerably among countries and are determined by how they are financed and managed. And it is worth remembering that health care, particularly in some African and Asian societies where traditional healers play strong roles, doesn't always fit the Western models.

Back in 1978, the World Health Organization announced its commitment to promote primary health care and many nations pursued this strategy, which resulted in smaller health-care facilities located near where people live. Decentralization necessitates a better flow of information, however, and many systems suffered because of their weak or even nonexistent infrastructure. In the United States, we've seen the increased use of ICT to deal with the increased complexity and rising costs. President Obama has highlighted the need for enhanced electronic medical records here at home. Based on 2005 statistics, electronic health record systems

PARTNERS IN HEALTH[10]

When patients, such as those with HIV, need care over long periods of time, medical records are crucial to their ongoing health. That's why Partners in Health (PIH) devised a web-based electronic medical record system in 2005 primarily to help track and treat HIV/AIDS and tuberculosis. Its open-source software enables the system to be widely accessible with limited funding. The central database allows clinical and administrative staff to track individual patients as well as monitor the patient population as a whole. Here's what they can now do:

- Accurately track patient outcomes.
- Enable more effective patient follow-up.
- Track patient identities and detect duplicate records.
- Store and analyze laboratory results.
- Provide decision support for prescribing medications and administering patient care.
- Better manage drug supplies.
- Generate reports for project management and funding agencies.

In Peru, thanks to PIH, web-based entry of tuberculosis laboratory results at all regional and central labs allows staff to perform tests with a system they call "e-Chasqui." More than 65,000 lab samples have been entered and tracked by e-Chasqui, and they hope to serve a network of institutions providing medical care for over 3.1 million people. What does e-Chasqui do?

- Connects labs and health centers by email
- Allows constant access of lab information to health center staff
- Provides tools for data quality improvement
- Generates reports for lab personnel
- Alerts clinicians to high-risk patients

Open MRS is fully customizable to perform almost any task. Rwanda started using it in August 2005, Lesotho in November 2006, and Malawi in late 2007.

(continued)

In addition to other features, the system accommodates a patient registry programmed to give reports that fulfill internal and national reporting requirements, a clinical tool that prints patient data and summaries on a daily basis, a database for operational research, and a drug prediction tool to assist in procuring medications. It provides a much fuller picture of each patient's care rather than lengthy paper trails that are likely to be lost or damaged.

Some of the challenges are:

- Data management/entry staff needs to be trained; one data clerk is needed for every 300 to 400 patient records and they recommend that a minimum of two data clerks are on staff at all times.
- Setting it up can be expensive.
- Software development and support require long-term resources and will necessitate collaboration with other organizations.
- Local buy-in is crucial to test systems on site.
- Local staff will need to be trained to use the system, to understand its benefits, and to actively participate.
- System upkeep is necessary; ICT staff requirements are that at least one technician per 40 computers at up to five project sites is needed for support.
- System security for prevention of viruses is vital to the safety and maintenance of the system.
- A stable power supply and battery backup is necessary to prevent loss of data. In Haiti, PIH has relied on generators but they recommend finding alternative energy sources such as solar, hydro, or wind power. Power spikes can seriously damage equipment and jeopardize the data. However, all the data is backed up on a server in Boston each night.

In collaboration with the Millennium Villages project, a joint effort by the Earth Institute, Millennium Promise, and the United Nations Development Programme to promote community-led development through knowledge centers, they intend to improve language capabilities beyond French, Spanish, and English and implement Spatial Patient Tracking using GPS devices to document patient locations.

are operational in only 12 percent of industrialized countries. So the need is even more dire in the developing world.

Electronic record keeping is useful for the following four areas:

1. Clinical care support
2. Reporting and analysis
3. Laboratory data management
4. Stock management

Taking steps to address this need, a nonprofit collaboration between the Regenstrief Institute and Partners in Health formed the Open Medical Record System (Open MRS) in 2004. It is an open-source framework for developing countries and is used now in many African countries. The Regenstrief Institute sponsors a National Library of Medicine (www.nlm.nih.gov), which is the world's largest medical library.

Partners in Health is a Boston-based nonprofit health-care initiative sponsored by Brigham and Women's Hospital and dedicated to reducing health disparities around the world.

ICT is essential for standardizing and making portable all sorts of patient data. It can segment patients by severity and sort out other salient health characteristics as well as offer inventory control.

TELEMEDICINE

Doctors in the United States began to use long-distance communication in the 1960s to bring medical assistance into rural areas as well as underserved urban areas. They used this to determine which patients need to be cared for at the most ideal tertiary care or specialty clinics. Because of health ICTs, thousands without immediate access to doctors have received needed treatment. It has also improved efficiency by reducing downtime and maximizing doctors' workload, along with reducing overheads. Not only are diagnostic technicians and specialists expensive and in short supply, but many are unwilling to work outside of urban areas. Telemedicine can bring needed health care to people in remote areas who never before could have afforded it, or been able to receive it. As Figure 2.2 shows, there

Teleradiology	The electronic transmission of radiological images from one location to another for the purposes of interpretation and/or consultation
Telepathology	The electronic transmission of microscopic digital images of pathological specimens between locations for the purpose of diagnosis/consultation
Telecardiology	The use of ICT to enable the practice of cardiology between geographically separated individuals
Telehomecare	The use of ICT to enable effective delivery and management of health services like medical diagnosis, treatment, and/or health maintenance between a patient's residence and a health-care facility or professional
Teleophthalmology	The use of ICT to remotely diagnose diseases of the eye
Telepsychiatry	The use of ICT to enable the practice of diagnostic psychiatry between geographically separated individuals

Figure 2.2   Types of Telemedicine

are many other needs that telemedicine helps to meet, ranging from radiology to home care.[11]

The University of Wisconsin and the Byrraju Foundation also created a low-cost network to expand health access into rural areas through a self-managing wireless mesh network that is also used for vocational and agricultural training, e-governance, and e-banking (examples of these are covered in subsequent chapters).

A HOSPITAL WITH AN EYE TO THE FUTURE[12]

Cataracts cloud the eye's crystalline lens; untreated, they can cause blindness. In India, as in many areas, about 90 percent of the population lacks access to trained ophthalmologists.

The Aravind Eye Care System in Tamil Nadu, India, began in 1976 as an 11-bed free hospital and is now the most productive eye care facility in the world, boasting an innovative financing and subsidizing plan that enables 2.3 million people to receive outpatient eye care in one year. The facility has performed 2 million surgeries in 32 years, and it screens 27 million patients each year. How is this done?

The business model the facility uses is "end to end," based on the goal of creating high-quality patient care at low cost throughout every stage of the process. The facility started what it calls the Aravind Teleophthalmology Network and built up numerous rural vision centers connected to the main Aravind hospitals by high-bandwidth wireless connections. This program has gone from pilot to a fully functional deployment of eye care for rural patients. Local people trained to conduct eye tests send the information to an ophthalmologist at the closest Aravind hospital via webcam. In some cases, the local staff will be given medical advice. In more severe cases, patients are referred to the main hospital for treatment. Because the eye hospital also has its own lens factory, service is low cost. Eyes and people are being saved with ICT.

Traditional telemedicine required a PC-based broadband infrastructure, which was too expensive for the poorer countries to afford. A new paradigm, where communication is via cell phone and two-way video is replaced by the ability to get accurate physiological data through sensors attached to the cell phone, offers a powerful way of reaching and treating otherwise-unreachable patients in ways never before imagined.

DIAGNOSIS AND PREVENTION

What is this illness? What caused it? Diagnostic technicians and specialists are expensive, in short supply, and often don't wish to work outside of urban areas. Therefore, over a three-year period, the External Research and Program Group at Microsoft funded the development of more than a dozen projects and experiments to show that cell phones can be equipped with medical sensors and networked to health professionals to provide basic diagnosis and triaged care as well as being coupled with pharmacies for an even broader range of health services.

DIALING FOR HELP: MOBILE PHONES CAN DIAGNOSE AND TREAT EMERGENCIES[13]

Mobile phones have a display, and they are widely used in India. Professor M. B. Srinivas of the International Institute of Information Technology in Hyderabad, India, asked the question: "Can we exploit this display to save lives?"

When a diagnostic device such as ECG costs as much as an average Indian yearly income, low-cost solutions must be sought. And given the fact that many people live in rural areas, often far from hospitals, transmitting diagnostic data quickly over WiFi or phones will definitely save lives.

So, Srinivas and his colleagues, backed by Microsoft Research, have created a low-cost diagnostic system for less than $100 that can be powered from a wall socket or by batteries. If a village owned one of these devices, capable of monitoring the electrical activity of the heart, including blood pressure and oxygen levels, they could get expert advice from a physician miles away, who could in turn instruct the local people what measures to take. It can also be adapted for other sorts of patient monitoring, such as for women with pregnancy risks and diabetes. They are partnering with COWs—the computers on wheels program in India whose mission is to expand Internet access to rural India. It's a timely device for use in villages that have Internet kiosks, but may not have a clinic.

> Current-generation mobile phones are more powerful than Pentium-based computers just a few years ago. In case of an emergency, the mobile phone can become a personal diagnostic device that includes a person's entire medical profile.
>
> —M.B. Srinivas, International Institute of Information Technology

By introducing ICT for health, we can address the high cost of trained health workers and lowering equipment costs along with providing more accessible devices. The following examples highlight the possibilities:

- You can put on "Health Gear," a monitoring device that Microsoft Research has developed using a camera and microphone. It can record blood flow, heart rates, and other signals, offering real-time analysis.

- The University of Botswana uses a similar device to monitor HIV/AIDS patients.
- The University of California promotes *telemicroscopy* for disease diagnosis by turning a cell phone into a quality microscope cheaply and efficiently. Images can be annotated, organized, and transmitted to experts for analysis and recommendations. The possibility of this device for use in poverty-stricken regions to provide early warnings of critical diseases is now a reality.
- The University of Buenos Aires is working on a "digital inclusion kit" to share patient data between educational and research communities in underserved areas of Argentina. By partnering with health agencies and the advanced technological expertise of funding partners, more applications are in the works, both for medical personnel for fieldwork as well as simpler kits for individual patient monitoring.

Phones for Health

Many physicians today rely on smartphones to combine their former pagers, PDAs, and cell phones all into one. It is likely that ultrasound imaging using smartphones will change global medicine.

Mobile phones are here to stay—and that's good for delivering better health care.

The Rwandan Minister of Health announced early in 2009 that they will be supporting their public health system using computers and mobile phones. They set out to establish a national electronic reporting system using Community Health Workers in mother-and-child health interventions. Using ICT, they will be able to send monthly reports and emergency calls at no cost. The government partners with the MTN (Mobile Telephone Networks) group, Accenture, Motorola, and Voxiva (a leading global provider of mobile-centric information and solutions that leverages mobile phones and their mConnect Services Platform). Voxiva, founded in 2001, is working with a wide range of partners such as Telecom Technology Channel, Global Health, and Global Development

MEDICAL IMAGING IN THE PALM OF YOUR HAND[14]

Twenty-first century medicine is defined by medical imaging, yet 70 percent of the world's population has no access to medical imaging. It's hard to take an MRI or CT scanner to a rural community without power.

—David Zar, Washington University in St. Louis, *Record*

William Richard and David Zar, both professors in computer science and engineering at Washington University, imagined a phone running Microsoft Windows as a complete computer. With a research grant from Microsoft, Zar wrote the phone software and firmware for the probes and Richard designed the probe's low-power electronics. The result was an ultrasound probe that worked with smartphones. Now David Zar, with one of the authors, Sailesh Chutani, has formed a company called Mobisante to commercialize this technology to make hand-held imaging a reality. Getting the price tag as low as $1 per scan is the goal.

You can carry around a probe and cell phone and image on the fly now. Imagine having these smartphones in ambulances and emergency rooms. On a larger scale, this kind of cell phone is a complete computer that runs Windows. It could become the essential computer of the developing world, where trained medical personnel are scarce, but most of the population, as much as 90 percent, have access to a cell phone tower.

—William Richard, Washington University in St. Louis, *Record*

It is now possible to build probes for imaging the kidneys, liver, bladder, and eyes; screening for cancers; and imaging veins and arteries for starting IVs and central lines. Trained people can send the images to a centralized unit where specialists can analyze the image and make a diagnosis. Medics could use them on battlefields to make better decisions about moving and treating patients. The applications are nearly unlimited.

Partners; they are able to deliver low-cost medical solutions in 13 countries in Asia and Africa, and in North and South America.

Even when people live in remote rural areas far from hospitals and lack health insurance, most have mobile phones. In Mexico, four-and-a-half million people can now consult with their doctors by mobile phone for a flat fee of about $5 a month. With funding from Fundación Carso, a charity funded by Mexican telecom magnate Carlos Slim, mHealth Initiative hopes to mine its data to benefit both patients and public-health officials. According to *The Economist*,[15] mHealth is already turning a profit and hopes to extend its services across Latin America.

An exciting area of development for Microsoft is partnering with Robertson Research Institute to further the use of artificial intelligence systems via an inexpensive feature phone. Their intended users: low- to midlevel health-care workers operating in remote and rural locations. These systems are readily adaptable to local and changing demographic and clinical dynamics.

REGIONALIZING MEDICAL DIAGNOSTICS FOR RURAL HEALTH[16]

Robertson Research Institute and the College of Human Medicine at Michigan State University have adapted an expert system of medical diagnosis for use by low- to midlevel health workers in remote and rural locations. Key to the successful deployment of this system will be the rapid adaptation of the database and clinical interface for use in specific regions and by varying user skill.

They developed NxOpinion—an expert clinical decision-support system—and adapted it for use by community health workers and laypersons. NxOpinion guides nonexperts to a probabilistic differential diagnosis through guided questioning followed by inference via a Bayesian network engine that mimics skilled clinical problem solving. Critical to this model is the ability to modify the resulting database in near-real time to address dynamic factors in rural and remote regions such as localization, seasons, and outbreaks, a process they refer to as *regionalization*.

In partnership with Microsoft, Robertson is field testing feature phones that access the network via cloud computing in Africa and Asia.

Providing Valid Prescriptions

Many governments have stockpiles of Tamiflu, for instance, to treat flu, but people still need valid prescriptions. Voxiva partners with Quinnian Health to provide Personal Protective Equipment (PPE). Quinnian Health provides health-care services and technologies with the aim of protecting clients from infectious diseases and other health threats. Companies can register their employees, who then take online health assessments so they can be prescribed and then are sent their appropriate medications and PPE.

Lowering Pregnancy Deaths

With mobile phones, trained community health workers (mostly women) can provide valuable services and make a real difference, especially where local cultural sensitivities may restrict male doctors from directly interacting with female patients.

Half of Nigeria's maternal deaths are due to postpartum hemorrhaging, which unskilled health workers lack the know-how or equipment to stop.

—Arabi Tukur, IRIN

According to an IRIN news report, "With an average of 5.5 births per woman, West Africa has the world's highest fertility rates, which puts women at greater risk of dying in birth, according to the UN Children's Fund (UNICEF)." Many babies are born to teenage mothers. Take Umar, for example. She lived in the northeastern state of Adamawa, Nigeria, and gave birth to her first child at 16.

By age 33 she was pregnant for the ninth time in a quest to deliver a prized male child, but following 36 hours of labor she bled to death, at home. None of Umar's nine children was delivered in the presence of a medical professional.

Umar's experience is common in Nigeria, where just 35 percent of births are attended by a skilled health professional, and one in 18 women dies in pregnancy or childbirth, according to the World Health Organization statistics.

"If a woman has more than four children, the fifth pregnancy can be more dangerous than the other pregnancies put together," said Ejike Oji, a gynecologist with the reproductive health NGO Ipas. Starting young also increases mortality, he said.

Many Nigerian women, particularly in the conservative north, give birth in their teenage years. But reducing early pregnancy can be tough given women's disadvantaged social position, according to UNICEF's latest State of the World's Children report.[17]

DISEASE SURVEILLANCE AND INFORMATION GATHERING

Communicable diseases, such as SARS or avian or swine flu, spread rapidly without proper intervention and the key to containing them is access to accurate real-time information. Early detection of epidemics can be crucial to containing their spread.

Ongoing systematic collection, analysis, and dissemination of health information improve health. But the real key is an increase not just in information and data, but in knowledge and how that knowledge is applied. It's crucial for epidemiology and decision making, particularly in areas with few other health resources. Not only can surveillance guide long-term planning, but it can help with impact assessments for emerging threats such as SARS, swine flu or any number of other threats we've encountered recently.

In many developing countries with the greatest health needs, the infrastructure for cellular phones is expanding rapidly, opening the door for greater use of cell-phone-based health-care devices. One team from Dartmouth College and their Vietnamese colleagues, for example, offer an electronic information system over a cell phone. This epidemiology network over a smartphone can bypass infrastructure constraints in Vietnam while providing much-needed medical information to users. It is easy to imagine that if such a system had existed in China during the SARS outbreak, it could have detected the epidemic much more quickly and hence led to actions that would have saved many lives.

Paul Meyer, founder of Voxiva, began a disease surveillance initiative—Alerta—in Peru in 2002. This health-service-provider company has now developed a back-end voice-recognition portal that allows health workers to submit patient and clinical data from anywhere in the region. The result has been better reporting of quality information without investment in infrastructure or technology at the edges of the network. They can gather real-time data from Web sources, telephone, fax, email, and SMS. Voxiva is responsible for technical issues and maintenance, not the clients, who simply interface with the system.[18]

In 2009, Canada's Alberta Health Services in the Edmonton area was using Voxiva's HealthWatch surveillance solution to monitor and detect possible early incidences of swine flu. Washington, D.C., also uses this application for early detection of flu outbreaks. After the 2004 Indian Ocean tsunami, multinational corporations (MNCs) in partnership with many Southeast Asian organizations have established a network of communications aimed at early detection.

Data mining and information retrieval is a core focus of ICT for health. For example, automated disease surveillance is done on the Web: from GPHIN to InSTEDD. InSTEDD (Innovative Support to Emergencies, Diseases, and Disasters) is a google.org-supported initiative to improve "early detection, preparedness, and response capabilities for global health threats and humanitarian crises."[19] It is based on the work of Harvard's HealthMap and Canada's Global Public Health Intelligence Network (GPHIN). GPHIN uses an Internet crawler to "scan thousands of websites in various languages for events and chatter recorded online on blogs, news sites, and other outlets that point to the early outbreak of diseases."[20]

The collective power of these tools and technologies is nothing short of revolutionary since they connect disparate data and information sources in order to build a holistic health picture, almost in real time. Perhaps more important, they provide the analytical ability to distill knowledge from data previously unavailable. Take, for example, the case of a pandemic.

"Any pandemic has the potential to create major disruptions in society," David Cerino, general manager of Microsoft Health Solutions Group, said. "Now more than ever, we are in a position to implement solutions to help people make better decisions during these outbreaks, such as social distancing, because of the technological advancements that companies like Microsoft have made over the past few years."[21]

Cerino is referring to a tool that allowed disaster-response teams in Mexico to monitor swine flu outbreak. The self-assessment licensed from Emory University is based on SORT (Strategy for Off-site Rapid Triage). The assessment reflects current public health and clinical science, vetted by a national network of experts from public health, clinical medicine, health education, and infectious disease. It is grounded in a clinical strategy endorsed by the American College of Emergency Physicians, the leading organization for emergency medicine in the United States.[22]

TAKING STOCK

As the many examples above illustrate, even some simple technologies available today can make a big difference when it comes to low-cost and effective diagnostic tools to identify disease, monitor and track disease progression, and offer reminders and compliance with other treatment regimes. We need to couple them with the right business models. Most of these business model explorations are currently happening in the developing economies, but the richer countries are paying heed in their own efforts to control costs and ensure adequate coverage. This is likely to be one of the areas in which we will see reverse innovation; that is, technologies and business models developed to meet the needs of the developing world will move to the richer countries to meet their needs of cost effectiveness.[23] There are models, such as that of the Aravind eye hospital, where the technology and business models both work. They are ready to be scaled worldwide.

The impact will be much bigger when the next generation of mobile-based telemedicine matures. This is an active area of research and development in universities as well as corporate research labs. We are now using more digital imaging and mobile technologies and

Web 2.0. And we're seeing more research in the areas of medical sensors to provide lower-cost diagnostic equipment attached to mobile phones. Whereas the focus in emerging markets is to empower health-care workers to deliver more and better care, in developed countries the same technologies are being used to put the consumers in charge of managing their own health. These different approaches

---

mHEALTH

In 2008 alone, over a dozen new mHealth programs have been implemented or are in trial stages. These programs leverage the power of mobile phones in order to provide health care. IRCD, a Canadian development agency, provides Caribbean nurses with PDAs to empower and improve diagnosis and decision making. And the World Health Organization, partnering with the Vodafone Foundation Technology Partnerships, is expanding mobile data gathering to more than 20 sub-Saharan African countries.

The year 2009 saw the launch of the mHealth Alliance, created by the partnership of the United Nations and the Rockefeller and Vodafone foundations, with the goal of encouraging mobile technologies in health care in the emerging economies (www .unfoundation.org/global-issues/technology/mhealth-alliance.html).

The National Institutes of Health in partnership with Microsoft Research held their first mHealth Summit (October 29–30, 2009, Washington, D.C.) to bring together the researchers and practitioners in this space. They are making this an annual event and have announced their intention to fund projects in this space as well.

The Bill and Melinda Gates Foundation has funded a few pilots in this arena as well, some of which are being spearheaded by Boris Nikolic, senior program officer for Global Health Discovery (www .gatesfoundation.org.).

mHealth involves using wireless technologies such as Bluetooth, GMS/ GPRS/3G, WiFi, WiMax, and so on to transmit and enable various eHealth data contents and services. Usually these are accessed by the health worker through devices such as mobile phones, smartphones, PDAs, laptops, and tablet PCs.

—Adesina Iluyemi, University of Portsmouth, United Kingdom

are a consequence of the disparate purchasing power. Individuals in richer countries can invest in more technology to trade off convenience and improve outcomes. The benefit is seen in reduced routine doctor and clinic visits, and hence lower costs overall. Using these technologies the patients can measure their vital signs at home, do routine testing, and let the doctor monitor their medications. They can also include their family and friends in the circle of care.

What all this means is that a new information architecture is emerging. It will make health care more accessible and affordable. One can imagine a future where millions of caregivers—midwives, physician extenders, or patients themselves—are equipped with sophisticated phones, medical sensors, and applications, and connected to the best experts and the resources of the Internet, where medical professionals can detect incipient epidemics in real time, and the doctors and pharmacies can get concrete data on which interventions are working and which aren't. That would be truly democratic access to health care, enabled by ICTs!

Of course, we are not there yet, but we can begin to take some steps to prepare for that future.

STEPS TO TAKE TO MOVE INTO THE FUTURE

Some necessary steps to take in order to move forward include:

- Exploring new business models.
- Creating positive feedback loops between global and local knowledge.
- Promoting pragmatic if unconventional collaborations.
- Seeking help from non-market forces to bootstrap the efforts.

Explore New Business Models

National health systems are strapped for resources and IT is often low on the list of priorities despite obvious and persistent gaps in the flow of information and knowledge within health systems. IT is about technology, but is more importantly about the improved processes brought about by the technologies. These improvements have been behind much of the gain in productivity that has taken place in the developed world. We need to rethink existing business models and develop new mechanisms for incentivizing the use of IT in health care. It needs to be clear to all participants that IT is not just a reduction to bottom-line profits but a generator of value within the health system. Examples of such work can be found in the Voxiva case; the system is positioned as generating upstream and downstream value. The Peruvian Ministry of Health is satisfied because they receive more accurate information on a more regular basis. The health clinics and medical facilities are content because they are no longer just passive transmitters of information but also receive summary statistics and other information valuable to their ongoing work. The medical staffs are fulfilled because the process of submitting data is streamlined and saves them time.

Most health systems in the developing world are decentralized national health systems, but the reality is that 75 percent of all patient contacts are with private health providers such as chemists and private doctors. Getting private providers to contribute to health IT is a considerable challenge, but one idea being considered is the use of special e-rates from technology and telecommunications companies for calling in patient information using a mobile phone or submitting data using a personal computer. Another is Grameen Telecom outfitting its successful operators with diagnostic equipment—thereby expanding on an already sustainable and successful model for service provision—to address a critical health need. The key takeaway is that it is crucial to the success of democratizing IT in health to develop novel business models that create incentives rather than disincentives to use these valuable technologies.

Create Positive Feedback Loops between Global and Local Knowledge

For ICT-based interventions to be effective, they have to create a two-way flow of information and knowledge between people and organizations. Here we need to recognize the mutual value of global medical, scientific, and technical knowledge, but also local expertise, experience, and wisdom. For example, local clinics and health workers need access to the latest research and medical knowledge, as well as connections to their peers. Local assets also have a tremendous amount of knowledge that they can contribute about unique diseases, clinical information, and best practices. Health care works best when practice and delivery are informed by knowledge, but the reality is that there is a deficit in knowledge and information management at the local level in developing regions. There is a need for IT-enabled solutions that target and utilize local assets in order to erase these deficits that can cripple the delivery of health-care services.

Promote Pragmatic if Unconventional Collaborations

Experiments and field deployments to date have relied on unconventional partnerships between individuals, researchers, MNCs, government, international organizations, NGOs, and so on. All of the experiments referenced in this chapter demonstrated the power of such collaborations in tweaking existing technologies, distributing new services, and testing potentially disruptive devices. These collaborations are necessary since the problems being handled are extremely complex and no single entity has all the expertise and knowledge required to solve them. These collaborations can improve the pace of learning and are likely to lead more quickly to sustainable solutions that work.

A partnership across sectoral alliances between the medical device manufacturers, pharmaceutical companies, and MNCs is needed. Consortiums that allow each player to offer its core competency will further efforts and prevent companies from innovating too far afield of their strengths. One working example comes from Pfizer's initiative to combat HIV/AIDS in Africa by leveraging NGOs. This pharmaceutical company engages in a number of actions to address the need to access drugs, including sponsoring the formation of the Infectious Disease Institute in Kampala, Uganda. While the initial impetus may be philanthropic, the local NGOs could help Pfizer discover the right business model that is also informed by the subtleties of the local context.[24]

Seek Help from Non-Market Forces to Bootstrap the Efforts

Given the limited purchasing power of the target segment, few MNCs are innovating in this space despite the large underserved markets. To avoid the increasing skittishness of many companies that suspend efforts before return is realized, we are starting to see unconventional partnerships extending the time horizon of MNCs. For example, in the case of health, international organizations, governments, and global foundations are pledging their support or providing initial subsidies to further development of health-care IT solutions for the masses. Acting as economic buyers in the absence of individual consumption in many of these markets will hopefully expand the proliferation of emerging-market technology innovation within and between industry players.

SUMMARY POINTS

- Small targeted improvements in existing technologies, especially mobile phones, are adequate to improve affordability and access to health-care services ranging from education to detecting epidemics.
- Innovation in smartphones, medical sensors that connect to them, and resources of Web 2.0 are giving rise to a new generation of mediators, à la barefoot doctors, to provide sophisticated diagnosis and triage services to underserved regions. The inherent cost advantage and coverage of this mobile infrastructure compared to PC- and broadband network–based models is making telemedicine viable and practical.
- Currently, most of the business model innovation is happening in the emerging economies, making it highly probable that reverse innovation will happen in health care. Sustainable

models that make health care affordable and accessible in the emerging economies are being used to address cost and convenience issues in the developed countries.

- Bootstrapping many of the health-care initiatives outlined here requires being open to tapping non-market forces and resources provided by social innovators, the NGOs, and the governmental agencies.

NOTES

1. Daqing Zhang and Paul U. Unschuld, "China's Barefoot Doctor: Past, Present, and Future," *The Lancet* 372(9653): 1865–1867, November 2008.
2. Jeffrey Sachs, *The End of Poverty: Economic Possibilities for Our Time* (New York: Penguin, 2005).
3. Allen L. Hammond, William J. Kramer, Robert S. Katz, Julia T. Tran, and Courtland Walker, *The Next 4 Billion: Market Size and Business Strategy at the Base of the Pyramid* (World Resources Institute and International Finance Corporation / World Bank Group, 2007).
4. Pop!Tech, "Project Masiluleke," www.poptech.org/project_m, (accessed July 26, 2010).
5. Text to Change, www.texttochange.org; Vital Wave Consulting, *mHealth for Development: The Opportunity of Mobile Technology for Healthcare in the Developing World* (Washington, DC and Berkshire, UK: UN Foundation–Vodafone Foundation Partnership, 2009).
6. Tessa Tan-Torres Edejer, "Disseminating Health Information in Developing Countries: The Role of the Internet," *British Medical Journal* 321(7264): 797–800, September 30, 2000.
7. Microsoft Research, "HealthLine Offers Speech-Based Access to Medical Information," http://research.microsoft.com/en-us/collaboration/papers/carnegie_mellon.pdf, 2007.
8. African Medical and Research Foundation (AMREF), "Upgrading 20,000 Nurses in Kenya," www.amref.org/what-we-do/upgrading-20000-nurses-in-kenya/, 2010.
9. Accenture, "Outsourcing: AMREF and Accenture: Working Together to Launch an Unprecedented E-Learning Initiative to Address a Critical Nursing Shortage in Kenya," www.accenture.com/NR/rdonlyres/84E3B47A-07E8-44D2-97BD-AA5EC4089E3B/0/AMREF.pdf, 2007.
10. Partners in Health, "PIH Model Online: Electronic Medical Records (EMR)," http://model.pih.org/electronic_medical_records, 2010.

11. V. Thulasi Bai, V. Murali, R. Kim, and S. K. Srivatsa, "Teleophthalmology-Based Rural Eye Care in India," *Telemedicine and e-Health*, 13(3), June 30, 2007.

12. Aman Bhandari, Mahad Ibrahim, and Jaspal Sandhu, "Remote Eye Care Delivery via Rural Information Kiosks" (white paper, Berkeley: University of California, 2004); Aravind Eye Care System, www.aravind.org.

13. Microsoft Research, "Portable Diagnostic Device Can Help Save Lives," http://research.microsoft.com/en-us/collaboration/papers/hyderabad.pdf, 2008.

14. Microsoft Research, "Ultrasound Imaging More Portable, Affordable with USB-Based Probes," http://research.microsoft.com/en-us/collaboration/focus/health/msr_ultrasound.pdf, 2008.

15. "A Doctor in Your Pocket," special report, *The Economist*, April 16, 2009.

16. Microsoft, "Medical Diagnostic and Treatment Software Holds Potential to Save Lives and Improve Patient Care Worldwide," http://microsoft.com/presspass/feautures/2004/jan04/01-21NxOpinion.mspx, January 21, 2004.

17. IRIN, "Nigeria: Childbirth Still Deadly," *Integrated Regional Information Networks*, www.irinnews.org/Report.aspx?ReportId=84689, June 3, 2009.

18. Voxiva, www.voxiva.com.

19. "Nonprofit InSTEDD Takes New Approach to Improving Global Health, Humanitarian Efforts, and Disaster Relief," http://instedd.org/news_launch (accessed August 26, 2010).

20. Roger Highfield, "Larry Brilliant, of Google.org: Internet 'Is Pandemic Early Warning System,'" *Telegraph* online, January 30, 2008.

21. "Microsoft Hosted Online Service to Help Flu Sufferers Seek the Right Medical Help," Microsoft News Center, www.microsoft.com/presspass/features/2009/oct09/10-15flualert.mspx, October 15, 2009.

22. PR Newswire: "Microsoft Launches Online H1N1 Flu Response Center to Support Consumers," www.prnewswire.com/news-releases/microsoft-launches-online-h1n1-flu-response-center-to-support-consumers-63664347.html, October 7, 2009.

23. Jeffrey R. Immelt, Vijay Govindarajan, and Chris Trimble, "How GE Is Disrupting Itself," *Harvard Business Review*, October 2009.

24. Pfizer, "Doing Business Responsibly," www.pfizer.com/responsibility/global_health/infectious_diseases_institute.jsp (accessed July 26, 2010).

CHAPTER 3

OUTSIDE THE "EDUCATION BOX"

WHO'S GETTING AN EDUCATION?

It's a simple fact: There will never be enough trained teachers to educate the world's children. There are not enough classrooms or appropriate textbooks, either. According to UNESCO, "there were 72 million children out of school in 2007. Business as usual would leave 56 million children out of school in 2015."[1]

> *The cost of educating children is far outweighed by the cost of not educating them. Adults who lack basic skills have greater difficulty finding well-paying jobs and escaping poverty.*
> —*Arye L. Hillman and Eva Jenker, "Educating Children in Poor Countries," International Monetary Fund, 2004*

Low school enrollments mirror regions with lower economic performance: East Asia, the Pacific, South Asia, and sub-Saharan Africa. Educational costs (school uniforms, books, transportation, and tuition) are often too high for the world's poorer families, who must instead place a higher priority on paying for food, energy, and shelter. Case in point: 44 percent of Angola's primary-aged children do not attend school. And a majority of them are girls, often due to financial, social, or physical barriers and pressures from high fertility rates, HIV/AIDS, and conflict.[2]

> *Today three out of every four girls in developing countries attend primary school. This is a vast improvement over what it was just a decade or two ago. When girls are educated, economic productivity improves, mother and infant death rates decline, families have fewer children, environmental management increases and the health, well-being, and educational prospects for the next generation improve significantly . . . Providing girls with one extra year of education beyond the average boosts their eventual wages by 10 to 20 percent.*
> — *Shannon Daley-Harris, Jeffrey Keenan, and Karen Speerstra,* Our Day to End Poverty

Even among those kids who are attending school, poor learning outcomes and low quality of education remain an overriding concern. In many developing countries, less than 60 percent of primary school pupils who enroll in first grade reach the final grade of schooling. The most recent Education for All (EFA) report has shown that 24 countries for which data was available had pupil/teacher ratios in excess of 40:1, and although this ratio had been gradually falling in much of the world, in sub-Saharan Africa this ratio had actually been rising consistently with a regional average of over 44:1.

Many governments often divert funds intended for education to the military or infrastructure. And when funds are provided, they are not usually evenly distributed. The richer countries represented by the Organization for Economic Co-operation and Development (OECD) spend over 6 percent of gross domestic product (GDP) on education while many developing countries are under additional pressure since the recent financial crises. According to UNESCO, "Sub-Saharan Africa faces a potential loss of around $4.6 billion annually in financing for education in 2009 and 2010, equivalent to a 10 percent reduction in spending per primary-school pupil."[3] Even though the World Bank increased its financing for education in 2009, costs are expected to rise to $12 billion.[4] As a result, most countries won't reach the United Nations' Universal Primary Education (UPE) goal by 2015. The numbers are grim when it comes to adult literacy as well; more than 20 countries have illiteracy rates in excess of 40 percent.[5]

Since there are simply not enough trained teachers, classrooms, and appropriate textbooks to go around, there has been an active interest in using information and communication technologies (ICTs) to bring access to education to the masses. Since the 1960s, radio and television have been used to overcome geographical boundaries and, more recently, computers and the Internet have begun to play important educational roles. Appropriate technologies can bring pertinent curriculum and teaching methods to people who are currently denied access to trained teachers.[6] Today's ICT has the potential to change pedagogical approaches within classrooms as well as play a larger role by increasing the reach of knowledge across geographic, social, and economic boundaries. However, this particular road, although paved with good intentions, is marked by more failed experiments and disappointments than successes. In order to not repeat those mistakes, it is critical to understand what works and what doesn't, and why.

BREAKING DOWN THE PROBLEM

It would be ambitious to try to describe the rich history of research, theory, and experiments in the field of education. But for the purposes of our arguments, here is an abbreviated attempt. Teaching and learning are separate and asymmetric activities. Learning is driven by the pupil. A lot of learning happens informally, outside of classroom settings for most people for most of their lives. Learning also happens by interactions with others who are grappling with the same issues, and by engaging in an activity whose mastery is desired.

Teaching is usually a professional activity, practiced by people with some sort of teaching credential. The teachers rely on a curriculum, which is either standardized or created by them or their colleagues. Formal teaching is also institutionalized in schools, colleges, universities, and such. Most teaching is also a one-to-many activity, where the teacher engages a large number of students at the same time in a classroom, an online forum, or similar venues. The outcomes are largely tied to a combination of quality of instruction, the curriculum, and student motivation. Modern education systems need trained teachers, standard curriculum, availability of infrastructure such as school buildings, and the requirement that students be present at the same time and place as the teachers. This creates large costs and makes education inaccessible to those who must work at the same time.

The cost of an education as shown in Figure 3.1 depends on where the education is provided (e.g., in universities, schools, or in people's homes) and who is providing the instruction (e.g., a university professor, a school teacher, or a trained intermediary). A university education provided by PhD professors is among the most expensive, whereas self-taught skills in home settings can be the least costly.

One way to increase access and lower costs is by relaxing the constraints of place and expertise required to educate people. As argued in *Disrupting Class: How Disruptive Innovation Will Change the Way the World Learns*,[7] it is at this juncture that ICT is beginning to have a major impact. Can ICT help deliver excellent curricula by

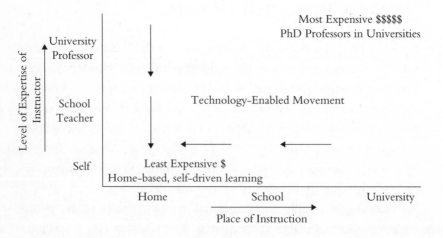

Figure 3.1 Making Education More Affordable

excellent teachers at a low cost and adapted to the unique learning style of every student? Are new innovations required to be able to do so? Can it be done in a sustainable manner? These are some of the questions whose answers we explore next. But first we would need to broaden our traditional focus on ICT training for technical literacy and employability. We would need to take a hard look at what works pedagogically and we would need to be open to creative business models.

THE CLASSROOM OF TOMORROW WITH TODAY'S TECHNOLOGY[8]

A computer science professor, Dr. Miguel Nussbaum, at the Catholic University of Chile moves beyond the traditional "skill-and-drill" educational formulas toward collaborative learning in which teachers guide students in exploring ideas and solving problems. While traditional methods might be efficient for teaching literacy, numeracy, and other basic skills, Nussbaum and others now find that by using handheld devices, mobile phones, and shared PCs with multiple mice, children have direct access to technology while enabling richer interaction with their peers.

> It is essential that the technological network support the social network—the students should be able to collaborate seamlessly. The students' face-to-face interaction should be the final aim, and the technology should be a transparent driving force.
> —Dr. Miguel Nussbaum

With support from the Microsoft Research Digital Inclusion Program, Nussbaum and a team of teachers, psychologists, designers, and engineers focus on educational approaches that are affordable and easy to build for schools in underserved communities.

Mobile phones, with nearly two billion worldwide users, are readily available to about two-thirds of Chile's 15 million residents. However, the current generation of handsets supports only text messaging and rudimentary email functions. They are also dependent on phone companies' networks, which are frequently quite expensive.

(continued)

Nussbaum and others realize that as richer functionality and WiFi networking capabilities work their way down, these barriers will disappear. However, they're not waiting.

They have developed wireless mesh networks that enable groups of phones or other mobile devices to run educational applications without relying on a server PC or the expensive phone network. Small groups of students can now use the small screen for software they have developed. They send multiple-choice questions to each student's phone. Working in groups of three, students discuss possible answers and enter their responses. If the answer is correct, they move on to the next question; if not, they continue working together until they get it right. Teachers can monitor and guide students with a separate mobile phone or Pocket PC, providing real-time feedback. A grid shows each group's progress.

Early trials in Santiago, Chile, show that students with mobile phones take personal responsibility for their learning. They also learn to work in close proximity, creating more opportunities to experience interaction and collaboration. They discovered it makes difficult subjects such as physics more accessible and enjoyable.

The team is expanding its trials to additional schools and plans to adapt its work to create a series of educational games. They will be conducting further experiments that combine wirelessly connected mobile phones, Pocket PCs and low-cost education devices such as Intel's Classmate PC to explore how a diverse range of devices can work together to improve learning outcomes.

With three children working together on a PC, each with a separate mouse, researchers learned that children 8 years or younger can more easily perform collaborative work sharing one screen than working on portable devices with small screens. By working in small groups of three, students are engaged in active learning. They collaborate, discuss, analyze, debate, and brainstorm. This kind of learning can have a powerful, immediate impact and help close the digital gap by eliminating the "digital cognitive divide" at an early stage.

> Computers and software are important cognitive devices that can help people nurture higher-order thinking skills. Cost shouldn't be a barrier to that kind of mental development.
>
> —Dr. Miguel Nussbaum

CLASSROOM ICT: A HISTORY OF UNMET EXPECTATIONS

Despite promising trends like Classrooms of Tomorrow, there is a long history of unmet expectations in ICT and education. We can agree that three fundamental justifications underpin most education and ICT investments, namely:

1. **Furthering human resource and skill enhancement.** ICT has gone from being primarily used for research and business to providing tools that pervade every aspect of our daily lives. Grasp of ICT is now as necessary as literacy.
2. **Enhancing productivity.** ICT is used to enhance productivity in different fields and it opens up all forms of knowledge via the Internet and the Web. Its mastery is required to remain economically viable and competitive.
3. **Pursuing our quest for quality learning.** ICT is versatile and has the potential to improve teaching and learning, including lifelong learning.[9]

The promise of transforming the learning process has been one of the greatest drivers of work in ICT and education, but perhaps the least realized so far. For decades, governments, donor agencies, and companies around the world have been vying to put computers in all schools, but all too often with little regard for outcomes. Many of the more promising low-cost computing projects such as the Massachusetts Institute of Technology's (MIT's) One Laptop per Child project or Intel's Classmate PC are primarily designed to serve younger school children and not the broader needs of students at all levels and life stages. The possibilities are endless, but we have let most educational technology fall victim to programs that are much like development programs from the 1950s, 1960s, and 1970s.

Take, for example, the Food Aid program in the 1970s, when the United States tried to help farmers in the developing world by giving them million-dollar tractors that ended up rusting in the fields. We thought we knew what people needed, but we missed the mark. We did not match our investments with the support actually needed on the ground. A similar thing has happened with ICT and education investments. Even while computer costs diminish, we still haven't offered enough high-quality software, programming, or support to those who need it. As a result, although our computers are not literally rusting in the fields, they are all too often locked up in schools or not used for their intended purposes. Their supporting ecosystem has often been nonexistent. When computers don't work, or students cannot access them, teachers, students, and parents become frustrated.

However, promising partnerships, programs, and learning from our mistakes can help "keep the tractors from rusting" and will create *real* learning tools for children and adults. We provide examples throughout the chapter.

CURRICULUM WITHIN REACH

ICT promises the possibilities of individualized learning and broadens the formal education windows of primary and secondary education, offering opportunities for continuing education and adult training. This relaxes the constraints of being in an institution in order to receive an education. High-quality curricula and high-quality teachers are key ingredients of successful teaching. Since great teachers are rare and high-quality curricula expensive to develop, one can increase access at low cost by distributing the instruction broadly through ICT. But it is not enough to just present the lectures; trained people are still required to mediate this content and help students engage with the content and with each other. ICT can help here as well as in assessing the student learning and outcomes. Because ICT itself is also a source of fascination, it can be the entrée into the broad field of science and technology for many. Take, for example, the free curriculum offered by one of the world's most prestigious universities, the Massachusetts Institute of Technology. Not only did other academic institutions follow suit, nonprofit entities like CORE (China Open

UNLOCKING KNOWLEDGE, EMPOWERING MINDS

"Free Lecture Notes, Exams, and Videos from MIT. No Registration Required."

In 1999, MIT faculty considered how to use the Internet in pursuit of MIT's mission—to advance knowledge and educate students—and in 2000 proposed OCW . . . MIT OpenCourseWare, a web-based publication of virtually all MIT course content. OCW is open and available to the world and is a permanent MIT activity . . . MIT published the first proof-of-concept site in 2002, containing 50 courses. By November 2007, MIT completed the initial publication of virtually the entire curriculum, over 1,800 courses in 33 academic disciplines.[10]

What Is MIT OpenCourseWare?

Although OCW is not an MIT education and participants don't receive a degree or certificate, students, self-learners, and educators all over the world can benefit from access to the materials. Take Kian Wah Liew, an educator in Malaysia. Liew is a secondary-school mathematics teacher in Kuala Lumpur who introduced his 18-year-old students to a range of complex concepts, such as matrices, determinants, and differential equations. Liew, who discovered OCW several years ago while searching the Internet for self-study resources in math and physics, uses OCW video lectures to supplement his teaching.

"OCW provides a chance for the students who never learned in an English-speaking environment to get an idea of how it would be when studying abroad," he says. In addition, Liew sometimes steers his most gifted students to other courses on the site to supplement their education. He says that OCW has been a very important resource to him: "The impact on my mind," he concludes, "has been great."

Resources for Education) and for-profits like Microsoft have published courseware in repositories as well.

Other efforts, such as iLabs, have been aimed at making expensive lab infrastructure available for remote manipulation and experimentation. The sheer richness of resources available on the Web, although not always easy to find or validate, is also making a dent. Collectively, these efforts are removing barriers and at the same time challenging the traditional business models of textbooks.

iCAMPUS: ANYWHERE, ANY TIME

The iCampus project was another example of technology crossing the boundaries of conventional education The project's home page on the MIT web site gives the following history:

> Initiated in 1999, iCampus was a research collaboration between Microsoft Research and MIT whose goal was to create and demonstrate technologies with the potential for revolutionary change throughout the university curriculum . . . More than 400 faculty and research staff and 300 students have participated in iCampus-sponsored projects—over 100 subjects in all.
>
> Areas of innovation resulting from the alliance have included using Web Services to enable a new educational information technology framework of software and services shared among universities worldwide; transforming the classroom experience by replacing traditional passive lectures with active learning experiences supported by information technology; and educational applications of emerging technologies such as speech recognition and pen-based computing.[11]

One important offshoot of the project was iLabs, an innovative approach to science learning.

> iLabs is dedicated to the proposition that online laboratories—real laboratories accessed through the Internet—can enrich science and engineering education by greatly expanding the range of experiments that students are exposed to in the course of their education. Unlike conventional laboratories, iLabs can be shared across a university or across the world. The iLabs vision is to share expensive equipment and educational materials associated with lab experiments as broadly as possible within higher education and beyond.[12]

When the iCampus experiment came to a close in 2006, MIT declared it a success:

> The MIT–Microsoft alliance has successfully done what it started out to do: It has fostered barrier-less collaborations and exciting new technological developments aimed at improving education in higher learning institutions, first at home at MIT, then globally, across borders, through its Outreach Initiative.[13]

The collaborative effort between Microsoft Research and the Massachussetts Institute of Technology shows again how a corporation and a not-for-profit organization can team up for the greater good.

CORPORATIONS INVEST IN ICT FOR EDUCATION

Multinational corporations (MNCs) are deeply engaged in the education space but have yet to crack the code. Nonetheless, major technology companies like Microsoft, Intel, and IBM continue to work toward real solutions to education problems through technology tools.

Microsoft has two of the largest corporate global initiatives around education and training through its Community Technology Skills Program (CTSP) and Partners in Learning (PiL) Program.[14] Since the Community Technology Skills Program began in 2003, Microsoft has provided more than $450 million in cash and software grants to more than 1,000 community partners. These donations have supported over 40,000 technology centers in more than 100 countries/regions. Microsoft is also recognized as one of the first corporations to acknowledge the importance of technology in advancing education goals, demonstrated by its research, philanthropy, and business efforts to date. Microsoft's Partners in Learning is a global initiative designed to help increase technology access for schools, foster innovative approaches to pedagogy and teacher professional development, and provide education leaders with the tools to envision, implement, and manage change. Since its inception in 2003, the Partners in Learning program has reached more than 90 million teachers and students in 101 countries with a combined financial commitment from the company for $500 million.

Microsoft is not the only company with a significant interest in this work; other major corporations have invested either research or philanthropic resources toward education and ICT initiatives, such as Vodafone (mobiles), Intel (chips), Google (Web Services), and IBM (services).

Vodafone

British telecom Vodafone has invested funds in information and communication technologies and development (ICTD) projects, both as research funding and as part of their corporate social responsibility (CSR) initiatives. Within research, Vodafone has been funding university fellowships and research grants examining the use of mobile applications in developing regions, in health care, and in education. As part of its CSR work, the company argues that extending affordable Internet access into emerging markets via mobile phones will help to bridge the digital divide, bringing information, communication, and educational opportunities to stimulate socioeconomic development. To tailor their services to emerging markets, Vodafone is developing low-cost handsets, implementing new business models, and introducing mobile transactions services. Vodafone has established local operating companies in Albania, Egypt, Romania, and Turkey, a presence in Kenya, South Africa, and other African countries through its affiliates and joint ventures, and new local operating companies in Ghana, India, and Qatar. Vodafone's earlier corporate responsibility initiatives were more oriented toward social concerns in Europe, where many of its earlier customers were; thus climate change, privacy, and Internet safety for children formed a major part of its past initiatives, and many of these continue to be important areas for the company.[15]

Intel

Intel has a keen interest in ICT and education from philanthropic and product development perspectives. In various parts of the world, Intel has been contributing free computers through the Intel World Ahead program, and through its Intel Teach program it has provided training on the use of technology to more than 5 million schoolteachers worldwide. Intel also has a "Computer Clubhouse" program bringing access to computers through kiosks or in after-school programs in over 100 centers in 20 countries. On the product side, Intel has invested in two different ideas. The first is Edu-wise, subsequently known as the Classmate PC, which is a small laptop for light use by students in the developing world. The second product is the Community PC, which is a ruggedized version of a PC designed for use in rough conditions. Recently, Intel has expanded offerings of its Learning Series to include a convertible "tablet" classmate PC, touch-screen interface, and rural connectivity platform.[16]

IBM

IBM's Education for a Smarter Planet projects have been very focused on skill-building at various levels, but are especially strong at the K–12 level. The projects for children, such as IBM KidSmart and Reading Companion, are oriented toward early childhood learning using technology—the program serves over 2 million children in 60 countries. The Reading Companion program is also oriented toward helping hone adults' literacy skills using speech-recognition technology. At the middle-school level, the IBM MentorPlace program (similar to Microsoft's employee volunteering program) provides online academic counseling in over 35 countries. In addition, IBM has programs encouraging science education among children, and support for girl children in technology, though these are more U.S.-focused. IBM also has the PowerUp program, a three-dimensional multiplayer game for classrooms.[17]

NEW DELIVERY METHODS

Even though they are not silver bullets, computers are a viable delivery mechanism for educational content targeting children. There are indications that poorer children can increase their math skills by using computers. School attendance has also been positively affected, along with parental interest in schooling that features computerized learning. We also know that younger children learn better through shared computer interactions with other children than they do from individual computer interactions. An innovative research project by Eduinnova in Chile, for instance, called "One for Three," uses one computer and three mice so three children can learn social skills, verbal language skills, and logical reasoning.[18]

Teaching and learning using Eduinnova's collaborative learning methodology is currently being implemented in Pirai, Brazil, which incorporates the use of one Classmate PC for every student in the city. "Pirai Digital" is a local governmental effort to democratize access to information technology and communications to generate economic and social opportunities for every resident of the city.[19]

PUTTING MICE TO WORK FOR LEARNING[20]

In most classrooms with limited computers, one child is "running things" and the rest are all passively standing by. The child using the mouse, usually the oldest or most dominant, is definitely learning things. But a child who has no mouse decreases engagement over time.

So, why can't all the children have a mouse? Up to the time Udai Singh Pawar, Joyojeet Pal, and Kentaro Toyama began asking that question, multiple mice were being used only in non-educational applications, and primarily restricted to two mice.

The economic benefits were obvious: a $100 laptop per child versus a $5 mouse. Even if the cost of the PC were $500, they figured if five children could interact, costs per student would still be around $100.

While Windows supports multiple mice, multiple cursors of different colors didn't exist in the way these researchers envisioned. They developed a toolkit that allows up to 15 cursors to work simultaneously. They did three trials in Bangalore, India, where all the children spoke Kannada. Their research centered around these key questions:

- Can children understand and use the multiple-mouse paradigm with as many as five mice?
- How do children interact with each other with respect to multiple mice? Do they share?
- Does the multiple-mouse paradigm increase interest and engagement?

"Now we don't have to fight for the mouse."
"Everyone can share."
"I'm green. I'm green. I'm green."
"She won. She's blue."
—Children in the multiple-mice trials

The results of their single-mouse versus multi-mouse trials showed:

- Children immediately understand the concept of multiple mice and multiple cursors.
- Children are not confused by multiple cursors on the screen.

- Children want to engage, but they want their own mouse.
- Girls tended to share; boys were more competitive.
- Children with mice remain engaged throughout.
- Overall engagement increases even for children without a mouse.

The authors of this study believe that when children work in small collaborative groups they are experiencing joint decision making and learning the skills needed in later life to interact with their peers in college or on the job.

Multiple mice in educational settings in developing countries can be a simple but very effective way of instantly multiplying the value of a shared computer in a school. The inherent simplicity in implementation and scaling is something we believe will go a long way in addressing the resource crunch that faces education in developing nations.

—Udai Singh Pawar, Joyojeet Pal, and Kentaro Toyama

In all of these efforts the high cost of computers and their supporting infrastructure continues to be a barrier. But there are creative ways around it.

The smartphones that people carry in their pockets in developing regions have more computing power than the PCs they may have had access to that are three or four years old. In fact, there are now more cell phones in schools than computers. The World Bank estimates that in India alone there will be 450 million cell phones by 2010. With smart mobile phones even people in remote areas will have access to an inexpensive yet sophisticated wireless computing device. Phones can be used for testing and tutoring. Software should most likely be created locally to meet specific educational needs, but local teams need investment help from the West to support quality programming. As one University of California, Berkeley, team discovered, smartphones may pave the way to literacy.

MILLEE (Mobile and Immersive Learning for Literacy in Emerging Economies) is a unique partnership between the University of California, Berkeley, led by Professor John Canny, and an Indian nonprofit organization, Suraksha.[21] It was funded by the Microsoft Research Digital Inclusion Program along with the U.S. National Science Foundation and an award from Qualcomm Inc.

> *The Microsoft Research funding has filled in one of the most difficult and crucial parts of the whole language-learning solution. It has allowed us to contribute to the body of knowledge about interface technology, and more generally, about how people who are illiterate or semiliterate can interact with information technology. We've created an open-source tool that many groups can use, and we expect to use it in other projects.*
>
> —*John Canny, University of California, Berkeley*

The Berkeley researchers set out to create an English-language-learning environment for children and decided cell phones offer an ideal platform because they are ubiquitous, affordable, compact, and wireless. In addition, children can see the alphabet, hear words spoken in English, and test their pronunciation.

In collaboration with Dr. Urvashi Sahni, who heads Suraksha, the team deployed and tested cell phone–based e-learning games in North India as a pilot program. Their research followed an earlier study involving 120 children in rural government and private schools and in urban slums that showed that game-play can produce significant learning benefits. The e-learning games concentrate on simple English-language skills such as vocabulary, phonetics, sentence composition, and spelling. These children tested significantly higher than children using traditional techniques.

The researchers hope to hand off a sustainable version of MILLEE for wider deployment, supported, ideally, by some combination of state education departments and telecom carriers. Further down the road, MILLEE researchers expect that the lessons learned in India will be applicable to other world languages, including Mandarin Chinese and Spanish, and will serve as a model for enhancing literacy in other developing countries in Asia, Africa, and Latin America.

EFFECTIVE MEDIATION

Once we have solved the problem of high-quality content and curriculum and an infrastructure for delivering them at low cost

DIGITAL STUDY HALL[22]

An obvious lack of qualified primary- and secondary-school teachers in rural areas prompted the "Digital Study Hall" project in 2004. This is a common problem seen in rural schools that are entirely managed either by a few overburdened teachers, juggling between classes and subjects, or by just one teacher. Furthermore, another problem in rural schools has been the shortage of technical teachers with competencies in mathematics and the sciences.

The Digital Study Hall identifies good teachers in rural areas, and records their in-class lectures. The recordings are collected in a repository and distributed through the postal system to schools where teacher shortages impede curricular instruction, especially in the sciences. Local personnel, who have some teaching and entrepreneurial abilities, mediate this content with the students. They can use television and video players, which are freely available everywhere. They show the lectures, help answer student questions, and stimulate discussion among students. By using local teachers speaking in the local dialects, the project seeks to maintain contextual relevance for children in rural schools. The larger idea behind the Digital Study Hall is that of a "people's database of everything"—as the project refers to itself. Think of combining YouTube, Kazaa, and Netflix with a local-language version of a school-curriculum Wikipedia, and you get the idea behind the Digital Study Hall.

This project has come out of Microsoft Research's Technology for Emerging Markets (TEM) lab in Bangalore, India, and has won the Association for Computing Machinery (ACM) Lawler Award.

to students anywhere, there still remains the vexing problem of finding teachers who can interpret the content, create a meaningful learning context, mediate with and between the students, and inspire them. Digital Study Hall, with its unique blend of low- and high-tech, offers a promising approach.

The Digital Study Hall project shows that high-quality educational content becomes more meaningful when mediated by someone, even if the person is not a highly qualified teacher. The Digital Study Hall model could be built up as a sustainable business by using a franchising model to equip local entrepreneurs to offer classes for small fees. This could work well and scale up since comparable efforts in targeted tutoring to prepare children for entrance exams to various universities are already successful in India and elsewhere.

WHAT IS KNOWN?

Through many experiments and some successful (and some flawed) implemented practices, we know ICT can extend access to education and positively affect learning outcomes.

Here's what else we know today about effectiveness of ICT in education:

- Math and foreign language acquisition show promise, but real impact is dependent on specific implementation and varies significantly.
- Children's school attendance can be positively affected, along with parental interest.
- Younger children can learn more effectively through shared computer interactions.
- Much of the time content for computer-aided learning in developing countries either doesn't exist or has been created without optimal design or pedagogical practices in mind.
- Typical usage scenarios for children in developing regions show three or more users on most ICT devices.

- Evaluation metrics are sketchy and problematic and often present contradictory results.
- Sustainability is often difficult to measure or estimate.

NEW DIRECTIONS AND CHALLENGES AHEAD

While we do have some evidence that points to how ICT positively affects learners, much of it is anecdotal, sketchily researched, or basically untested and therefore hard to quantitatively prove because so many other factors are present. How competent is the teacher? Does the teacher have adequate time and materials? What cultural barriers prevent a child from learning? How regular is the student's attendance? Do the parents fully support the child's education? Is the curriculum or software programming fully tested and robust? Does the material match the culture? Are the IT devices fully supported and administered?

Little solid published research exists relating to ICT's impact on education in developing regions. However, some early documents help us grasp an idea of what to watch for in the future. To date, most IT tools used in education in less-developed countries support existing teaching and learning practices. There are some recent exceptions (for instance, the research out of Catholic University in Chile in teacher ICT training), but usually IT devices extend what is already practiced in the curriculum.

There are emerging best practices and lessons learned in a number of areas, but with a few exceptions (such as SchoolNet[23]) they have not been widely disseminated or packaged into formats easily accessible to policymakers and practitioners in developing countries and have not been explicitly examined within the context of universally held educational goals such as those established by UNESCO (United Nations Educational, Scientific, and Cultural Organization).

While the rhetoric of public–private partnerships has been strong throughout the 1990s, there is little evidence today that broad ICT field operations and implementation have been widely successful. What evidence does exist may not always paint a full picture. For instance, a survey of research on ICT and education shows there is countervailing evidence that may suggest computers do nothing significant to help children learn better math and may even push mathematical ability backward.[24] Likewise, we find equally contrarian evidence on language, making it unclear whether computers actually assist, impede, or fail to have any impact on language acquisition and development.[25] Much anecdotal evidence exists, including teachers' observations of increased confidence in children and their enhanced group efforts. This, of course, breeds optimism for future efforts, but hard evidence regarding overall quantitative leaps forward has yet to be garnered. The future is open to much-needed solid research.

We need to approach the future with our eyes wide open to the barriers that exist, as well as the vast potential that awaits students around the world.

Physical and Economic Constraints

Given the present economic picture, most educational systems around the world are reeling under the pressure of basic costs. Although some communities, as we have shown, are attempting to provide computer access to all children, the reality of one computer for each child is still a far-fetched notion, especially in view of ongoing costs of keeping computers running with updated software and pertinent curriculum. Mobile phones are, however, emerging as a viable and inexpensive computing platform that is also affordable.

Keeping networks accessible and available, particularly in remote regions, poses even greater challenges because they are usually part of a national infrastructure. Access is often narrow, unreliable, and poorly funded.

Social and Cultural Constraints

Many teachers and parents are not familiar with computers or newer technologies. Therefore, teacher training must become uppermost in a region's plan to upgrade education. Some regions, because of nationalism or religious or other cultural beliefs, are resistant to using devices and programs brought in from beyond their borders. To be widely accepted, local professionals must, ideally, produce educational curricula, software, and videos using people and examples from that particular culture. Imposing Western culture has been tried, historically, and failed. Western research tempered with local insights has shown degrees of success, particularly in India, where much research has already been conducted.

Evaluation

All educators grapple with metrics and return on investment (ROI). Measuring what a student has learned, grading students, evaluating people who come from diverse backgrounds is extremely challenging. Because it's hard to evaluate the benefits of computer-assisted learning, for instance, people have contradictory expectations of ICT in education. Policymakers and technologists generally sit on the optimistic end, whereas economists typically take a more skeptical view of the quantifiable benefits. Finding the right evaluation metrics based on a more holistic concept is key to future successful projects, rather than continuing to cling to the traditional expenditure/outcome measurements.

Scaling

How to bring small successful pilot programs to the larger real-world arena is a question both academic and industry leaders grapple with. Within industry and policy circles, suggestions for overcoming the challenges of appropriate scaling have primarily involved capacity building and entrepreneurship development. In academic circles, people struggle with how to strengthen evaluation metrics as a means of supporting scaling. Few if any of the experiments have transitioned from proof-of-concept pilots to at-scale deployments or sustainable businesses.

Content Development

Most computer-aided-learning digital content in the developing world consists of *narrative-interactive loops*, which present material in a digital format and then follow it with multiple-choice modules or some equivalent method of testing.[26] All too often this material is directly translated from existing content in other countries, usually from the West, or else directly taken from existing school curricula or training pamphlets. People doing this often lack sound digital pedagogy. One of the key focus areas of ICT in education must be building local capacity among leading educators and teachers. The Digital Study Hall project is a strong step in that direction. Digital content is too often provided by technical and design experts without input from the teachers themselves. However, teachers are unlikely to be able to be the primary content providers. Recognizing this, it is important to design curriculum to train and certify learning material experts with nongovernmental organizations (NGOs) or design firms that specialize in digital content creation—particularly for today's hand-held devices.

Both the platforms and the content of computer-aided learning pose serious challenges for the future. Platform issues pose both business and compatibility challenges. Both Windows- and Linux-based systems are widely prevalent in developing regions, but the content is often designed for either one or the other with the lack of cross-platform compatibility being a very serious problem. Shared computing platforms have shown exceptional promise in the developing world and children do learn better in shared-use situations. The technical challenge before us now is how to redesign existing material for multiple users and how to structure licensing for such scenarios.

Sustainability

As we ponder the challenges that lie before us, we need to consider how to sustain promising projects as well as how to ensure the quality of the educational products once we expand access and opportunities. By experimenting and through trial and error we have learned that sustaining education and ICT projects in diverse environments poses real challenges. We have had difficulty in accurately estimating costs primarily because of the variable investment needs of training and maintenance. For projects designed on a "build-operate-transfer" model, even with needed initial subsidy components, communities have often been unable to purchase them because they are too expensive once the initial subsidy plan expires. Education projects in Brazil and India have proven this to be the case.[27] In general, economic self-sustainability does not work.

Client-paid services for educational ICT may be structured on the wrong model. Educational services are expected to be free. People are reluctant to pay, particularly in public schools. Because of wide variations in people's poverty levels, it is often very difficult to make region-wide generalizations about who will be willing— and able—to pay for what.

Perhaps we need to view sustainability through another lens. What if we considered sustainability for ICT in education based on usage? What if the metric were the continued use of the service, irrespective of people's ability to pay for it? We have noted usage sustainability in younger children. The challenge in considering continued usage as a metric is that it relies on the teacher's willingness to promote the ICT pedagogy as well as the reliability of infrastructure such as electricity and networks.[28]

The challenges surrounding education plague every society, but the challenges in developing regions are even more compelling. Over the past few years, much of the earlier hype about technology being "the answer" has been tempered. We now see a more balanced set of hopes centered on what is reasonably possible given realities in the various fields. The pace of experimentation has picked up just as there is broad consensus that we have to solve this problem urgently in order for economic development to take place. These are ripe conditions for a truly disruptive technology, pedagogy, or business model to emerge.

SUMMARY POINTS

- High-quality, affordable education is one of the most promising ways of enhancing the lives and the value of developing countries' best resources—their people.

- Despite early failures, ICT has the potential to increase the affordability and reach of education. Enough evidence is emerging that shows what works and what doesn't.
- A more formal and rigorous assessment of the impact of ICT and the return on investments will help overcome the justifiable skepticism of policymakers and educators.
- ICT can enable low-cost creation and distribution of high-quality content, its delivery, and its mediation by trained entrepreneurs.
- The biggest lacuna today is in scaling the proof-of-concept prototypes into sustainable businesses that have a broad impact.

NOTES

1. UNESCO. *Education for All (EFA) Report* (Geneva: UNESCO, 2010).
2. Ibid.
3. Ibid.
4. Barbara Bruns, Alain Mingat, and Ramahatra Rakotomalala, "Achieving Universal Primary Education by 2015: A Chance for Every Child," The World Bank, http://go.worldbank.org/F30T33DI80, 2003. See also www.worldbank.org/education.
5. UNESCO, *Education for All (EFA) Report.*
6. UNESCO, "Information and Communication Technology in Education: A Curriculum for Schools and Programme of Teacher Development" (France: UNESCO Division of Higher Education, 2002).
7. Clayton Christensen, Jerome H. Grossman, and Jason Hwang, *The Innovator's Prescription: A Disruptive Solution for Health Care* (New York: McGraw-Hill, 2008).
8. Microsoft Research, "The Classroom of Tomorrow, Built with Today's Technology," http://research.microsoft.com/en-us/collaboration/papers/chile.pdf, 2007.
9. Pedro Hepp, Enrique Hinostroza, Ernesto Laval, and Lucio Rehbein, "Technology in Schools: Education, ICT and the Knowledge Society," World Bank, www.worldbank.org/education/pdf/ICT_report_oct04a.pdf, 2004.
10. Massachusetts Institute of Technology, "MIT Open Courseware," http://ocw.mit.edu/index.htm (accessed July 26, 2010).
11. iCampus: The MIT–Microsoft Alliance, "MIT iCampus 1999–2006," http://icampus.mit.edu, January 8, 2007. See also Stephen C. Ehrmann, Steven W. Gilbert, and Flora McMartin, "Factors Affecting the Adoption

of Faculty-Developed Academic Software: A Study of Five iCampus Projects," TLT Group, 2006.

12. iCampus: The MIT-Microsoft Alliance, "iLabs: Internet Access to Real Labs—Anywhere, Anytime," http://icampus.mit.edu/ilabs, March 29, 2005

13. iCampus: The MIT–Microsoft Alliance, "MIT iCampus 1999–2006."

14. Microsoft, www.microsoft.com.

15. Vodafone, www.vodafone.com.

16. Intel, www.intel.com.

17. IBM, www.ibm.com.

18. Eduinnova, www.eduinnova.com.

19. Esther Andrews, "A 'Positivo' Milestone for Intel-Powered Classmate PCs!" *Technology@Intel*, http://blogs.intel.com/technology/2009/06/a_positivo_milestone_for_intel.php, June 17, 2009.

20. Udai Singh Pawar, Joyojeet Pal, and Kentaro Toyama, "Multiple Mice for Computers in Education in Developing Countries," ICTD 2006 Conference Program Proceedings, May 25–26, 2006.

21. Microsoft Research, "Mobile Language-Learning Tools Help Pave the Way to Literacy," http://research.microsoft.com/en-us/collaboration/papers/berkeley.pdf, 2008.

22. "Digital Study Hall," http://dsh.cs.washington.edu (accessed July 26, 2010).

23. SchoolNet Africa, www.schoolnetafrica.org.

24. H. Wenglinsky, "Does It Compute? The Relationship between Educational Technology and Student Achievement in Mathematics," *Educational Testing Service*, 1998; J. Angrist and V. Lavy, "New Evidence on Classroom Computers and Pupil Learning," *The Economic Journal* 112(482): 735–765, 2002.

25. L. Barrow, L. Markman, et al. (2007). "Technology's Edge: The Educational Benefits of Computer-Aided Instruction," Federal Reserve Bank of Chicago Working Paper 2007-17, 2007.

26. Joyojeet Pal, Udai Singh Pawar, Eric Brewer, and Kentaro Toyama, "The Case for Multi-User Design for Computer Aided Learning in Developing Regions," Proceedings of the 15th International Conference on the World Wide Web, 2006.

27. C. Ferraz, R. Fonseca, J. Pal, and M. Shah, "Computing for Social Inclusion in Brazil: A Study of the CDI and Other Initiatives," UCB-UNIDO Bridging the Divide Conference, May 2004.

28. T. Scott and M. Engel Cole, "Computers and Education: A Cultural Constructivist Perspective." *Review of Research in Education* 18: 191–251, 1992; Joyojeet Pal, "Early-Stage Practicalities of Implementing Computer Aided Education: Experience from India," TEDC2006: Fourth IEEE International Workshop on Technology for Education in Developing Countries, 2006.

CHAPTER 4

MICROFINANCE

The Next Phase

WHO ARE THE "UNBANKED"?

The unbanked includes anyone without access to formal financial services. According to the World Bank, nearly three billion people, primarily in developing countries, lack adequate ways to access money.[1] Ethiopia, for instance, has less than one bank branch for every 100,000 people. And just to open a checking account in Cameroon, you have to pay the bank $700.

Many countries and populations experience financial risk due to relatively low levels of traditional financial access.[2] What do you do if you can't get a loan? You often have to turn to predatory lenders who charge exorbitant rates and you're never sure whether your money is safe, devalued, or stolen.

Many people live far from real banks and, even when they can reach one, they may be turned down because they're asking for too little for the bank to process, or they lack the necessary documentation, or they can't read or write, or the costs of transactions are beyond their limits.

Access to financial services can be a first step in breaking out of the gripping cycle of poverty.

MICROFINANCE: MEETING FINANCIAL NEEDS OF POOR HOUSEHOLDS

Microcredit enables people to profit from their work and leave poverty behind. It can help us meet Millennium Development Goal 1 of eradicating extreme hunger and poverty and its target for 2015 of reducing by half the proportion of people who earn less than $1 a day.

—Shannon Daley-Harris, Jeffrey Keenan,
and Karen Speerstra, Our Day to End Poverty

Microfinance offers credit in the form of small loans to help the poor build their own resources and become less vulnerable. It also empowers women and families by helping them to secure better education for their children and health care. Microcredit accounts allow people to purchase seeds, pay school fees, and protect against emergencies such as natural disasters or death in the family. It empowers women and allows children to go to school.

In the 1970s, early microfinance efforts, upon which today's microfinance institutions are based, began in Brazil, Bangladesh, and a handful of other places. Today, microfinance institutions serve about 160 million people in developing countries.[3] While this may seem like a significant outreach, the majority of the countries where microfinance is active have an average outreach of only 2 percent of the population (not including a few countries like Bangladesh, which have an outreach of 21 percent of the population).[4]

As microfinance becomes a more popular method of providing financial services to the poor, more organizations and businesses are entering the marketplace to compete in what is becoming a fast-growing industry. In 2006, Africa, the least developed region in terms of microfinance, saw a large increase in outreach of the

GRAMEEN[5]

The most celebrated early microfinance example is Professor Muhammad Yunus and the creation of Grameen Bank in Bangladesh. In 1976, Professor Yunus loaned a group of 40 women in a neighborhood of Dhaka the equivalent of $27 with the one request that they must pay the money back when they were able to. After receiving his money in full, he set out on a quest to make financial services available to the poor and that trend has grown globally.

By the 1990s, bank officials wanted to offer financing to higher-yield businesses and capture some of the benefits from the emerging technology sector. So they established a nonprofit company called Grameen Telecom as well as a for-profit called Grameen Phone Ltd. Now, all the "Village Phone" project needed was women to operate cell phones as a business. The women needed to have been Grameen Bank members with a stellar repayment record, to have access to electricity to charge the phones, and to be centrally located. They each get a loan (repayable in three years) to purchase their cell phone for approximately $420. They become phone operators, providing phone services to villagers at a market price per call. On average, 70 customers per month use the phone to transact business or stay in touch with family and friends at a much lower cost to them than having to travel to a phone somewhere beyond their village.

Grameen Phone now has over 20 million subscribers and a network that covers about 98 percent of the population and land area of Bangladesh. They have 5,000 full-time, part-time, and contractual employees and another 100,000 are dependent on Grameen for their livelihood.

In addition, Mifos is Grameen Foundation's award-winning software for microfinance institutions. Mifos is part of the Technology for Microfinance Initiative, based at the Grameen Technology Center in Seattle, Washington. Mifos offers a flexible technology solution to more efficiently and effectively deliver financial services to the poor. Currently, the software is being used in production by eight microfinance institutions across India, Tunisia, Kenya, Philippines, and Senegal, serving more than 550,000 clients.

microfinance sector across the continent, from 3.1 million borrowers to 3.8 million.

The average market penetration rate (number of borrowers per number in poverty) for countries engaged in microfinance is a mere 7 percent. Leveraging technology will be critical for microfinance institutions (MFIs) globally to achieve scale and increase this market penetration.

Different types of financial services—from deposit services, to money transfers, to credit and insurance—are fundamental tools for managing a poor family's well-being and productive capacity. Often their incomes are erratic, with only occasional work or seasonal crops.

Small loans are what they need, and Muhammad Yunus, founder of the Grameen Bank in Bangladesh, received a Nobel Peace Prize in 2006 for figuring out how to do just that.

MICROFINANCE GOES BEYOND THE "LENDING CIRCLE" APPROACH

Traditionally, microfinance was the purview of the nongovernmental organizations (NGOs), cooperatives, and small rural banks and the donors that funded their work. They originally had a narrow geographic focus, provided loans to a specific demographic, and relied heavily on donations to sustain their lending programs. The programs focused almost exclusively on providing small loans (often less than $150) to the poor for the purpose of starting an income-generating project. But over time, they have proven very innovative, pioneering banking techniques like solidarity lending, village banking, and mobile banking that have overcome barriers to serving poor populations.

> *Microfinance is about building local financial markets that meet the diverse financial services needs of poor people.*
>
> *— The World Bank*

Today's understanding of microfinance goes beyond small loans to individuals to providing relevant and affordable financial services to poor households. Research shows that providing bank services is not only "pro-poor" but it is also "pro-growth," and countries with better developed financial systems experience faster reductions in income inequality and poverty.

Microfinance means more than providing small loans for small business. It includes a broad range of financial services, including deposit services, money transfer services, and micro-insurance. Take, for example, major players in the microfinance movement: ACCION of Venezuela and Bangladesh Rural Advancement Committee (BRAC), which have led microloan activities for decades but have diversified beyond core constituencies and geographies. Started in 1961, ACCION now has a network of lending partners that span Latin America, Africa, Asia, and the United States. The village organizations of BRAC even combine microfinance with other needed social interventions in agriculture, community development, nonformal education, adult literacy, and health care. BRAC has even grown to include BRAC University and BRAC Bank, both started in 2001.

SKS USES TECHNOLOGY TO TARGET PEOPLE AT THE BOTTOM OF THE PYRAMID[6]

What would happen if you could eradicate poverty by using modern, efficient back-office systems to lower banking transaction costs and offer people an opportunity to get loans if they need them? Vikram Akula, recognized as one of today's most influential people by *Time* magazine, answered that question in 1998 by founding SKS Microfinance. Its purpose: to empower the poor to become economically self-reliant and to do it in a sustainable manner. SKS currently has branches in 18 states and offers services to 4.5 million

(continued)

female clients throughout the poorer regions of India. Its goal is to reach 15 million clients by 2012. Borrowers who have shown credit discipline take loans for all sorts of endeavors, including raising livestock, vegetable vending, basket weaving, pottery, beauty parlor businesses, and photography. This is all delivered through a Grameen (village) banking program developed by Grameen Bank of Bangladesh. It offers interest-free loans for emergencies and life insurance for its clients. An affiliate, SKS Education, provides education services to poor children.

SKS is so tuned in to specific local needs that when loans for buffaloes rose rapidly, for example, it quickly responded by finding borrowers in such areas as retail, construction, and vehicle repair to sustain that growth. The success of SKS is reflected in big banks lining up to lend it funds. SKS has a 98 percent on-time repayment rate and earns a higher return on capital than other banks' large corporate borrowers.

At the heart of SKS is its information system technology platform that allows transactions to be made efficiently and at lower costs. An online data transfer system allows all branch-level transactions to be consolidated and compressed and sent over a dial-up connection in less than two minutes over the Internet.

SKS believes that the future of microfinance will be shaped by innovative microfinance informational systems (MIS) technologies— and they are poised to be the global leaders in this effort.

BARRIERS TO MICROFINANCE

If microfinance is such a great idea, why don't we see more of it? There are several reasons. MFIs and the clients they serve have not been part of the formal banking system and have operated outside of it. Only recently are we seeing major banks lend to MFIs, which in turn lend to the poor. Financial institutions usually make loans to people who have good credit history and some asset base that can be used as collateral against the loans, and to those whose needs are large enough that the bank can make good profits while meeting their needs. The institutional and the professional infrastructure have evolved over the centuries with this model in mind. However, the poor segments of emerging economies, especially those making $1 to $2 a day, rarely have a credit history, their needs are for small amounts of money, and they usually do not have any asset base to speak of. This means that the traditional banks do not find it attractive to go after that segment.

Banks incur substantial fixed costs to manage a client account, regardless of the amount involved. For example, the total profit from delivering 1,000 loans worth $100 each will not differ greatly from the revenue that results from delivering one loan of $100,000. But the fixed cost of processing a larger number of loans is much higher. These costs are incurred as part of the assessment of potential borrowers, their repayment prospects and security, administration of loans, and costs of delinquency. There is a breakeven point in providing loans or deposits below which banks lose money on each transaction they make. Poor people usually fall below it.

Just as in the case of health care and education, the inherent cost structure of banking is determined by where the activity takes place and the level of expertise required to carry out the activity, if the cost and availability of capital is fixed. Typically it is institutions such as banks that extend the loans with the help of the professional staff of bankers who are trained to assess risk. As illustrated in Figure 4.1, one way of making credit more broadly available is to reduce the cost and complexity of institutions and professional expertise required to make loans profitably. Information and communication technology (ICT) offers some ways to do that. It can dramatically reduce transaction costs by not requiring "bricks-and-mortar" infrastructure or even expensive ATM machines. For example, an ATM transaction can cost $0.15 to $0.50 compared to $1 to $2 for a teller transaction. And an Internet transaction costs only $0.01. ICT can reduce the level of expertise required to assess and manage risk, both by exploiting local knowledge and by making powerful analytical tools available to the local entrepreneurs. It can also match up those with capital with those who need it.

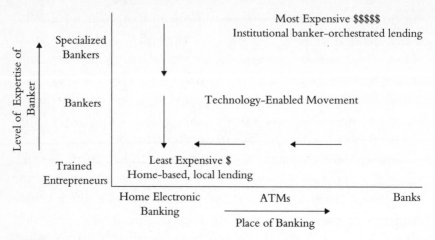

Figure 4.1 Making Finance More Affordable

The banking sector is also highly regulated by the government. As new entities emerge to provide "alternative banking" possibilities for the poorer segments, the lines between traditional banks, telecommunications companies, and NGOs become more blurred. Commercial banks are increasingly providing microfinance services by partnering with mobile phone companies, so technology corporations are now finding roles within microfinance. One of the best examples of this is the emergence of M-Pesa in Kenya (see the "Money in a Phone" case study later in this chapter.)

ICT IS HELPING

ICT is reducing the cost of financial transactions by enabling lower-cost phone-based transactions, by leveraging new modalities such as smart cards, by enabling low-cost franchising, and by making it easier to match up those who have capital with those who need it.

Lower Cost Channels

Some financial institutions are beginning to expand their financial services to more remote locations by leveraging ICT to replace the traditional banking center. As Figure 4.2 shows, ICTs are

Technology Channel	Number of Institutions
ATMs	46
Point of Sale (POS)	35
Internet Banking	26
Mobile Phone Banking	10

Note: 62 institutions in 32 countries—75 percent institutions in large markets (India, Brazil, South Africa) and small markets (Malawi, Namibia, Guatemala)

Figure 4.2 ICT Channels Used by Financial Institutions

Source: Gautam Ivatury, "Harnessing Technology to Transform Financial Services for the Poor," ITDG Publishing, December 2004.

increasingly making it possible to provide banking services to people in remote rural areas with the help of mobile phones or smart cards that carry the financial history of the client. Whereas these technologies are being deployed primarily as pilot projects, many of them have tremendous potential. In the short term, they have provided a low-cost additional channel.

At some point in financial transactions, real cash has to be disbursed. This poses another problem for banks. Transporting cash between remote locations and banks is hazardous, risky, and inconvenient for all parties involved. In order to overcome some of these problems, ICICI, a bank in India, has taken up the task of creating a low-cost ATM that will allow its customers to carry out cash transactions.[7] The ATMs will have a graphical user interface that makes it easy for the client to carry out the transaction. This ATM can hook up with the corporate information systems periodically, depending on the connectivity of the system. The ATM is supported with either a magnetic card or a smart card that is given to the client. This card can carry the client's information, allowing her to carry out transactions once she swipes the card. While magnetic cards are cheaper, smart cards have offline functionality that can be key in remote areas not connected with the Internet and also are considered to be more secure.

In order to reduce the costs even more, a leading technology institution in India, IIT Chennai, is in the process of creating low-cost ATMs with fingerprint recognition that can be used by

MFIs. Fingerprint recognition completely removes the need for investing in any kind of smart card or electronic card and allows the client to access her account.

INDIA

India is considered to be the largest microfinance market in the world, characterized by the world's second largest population, a concept of microfinance that has existed for 30 years, and an entrepreneurial culture that is conducive to effective loan utilization. It is estimated that there are currently 37 million borrowers; this number is growing at a rate somewhere between 30 and 40 percent per year. While India does have a robust banking and financial system, a majority of the more than 70 million households living below the poverty line in India do not have access to financial institutions. It is estimated that only about 20 percent of the population of the country has access to credit from the formal sector. This leaves a gap for microfinance institutions to fill.

The microfinance industry in India has been emerging since the 1990s and has been led by NGOs. It is based largely on two models: the Self-Help Group (SHG) bank linkage model and the Microfinance Institution model. Microfinance in India is largely limited to microcredit. Due in part to regulatory reasons, savings and insurance and other tools in microfinance have not been able to grow as much.

A few notable MFIs, such as Grameen Koota and SKS, have supported phenomenal growth levels through increased Internet connectivity and tools that can be utilized with it, such as centralized online MIS and hand-held devices in the field. The use of mobile phone technology holds strong potential for further lowering costs and increasing efficiency and outreach to poorer rural clients.

A final important characteristic of the India market and technology is that many MFIs have at their fingertips a population of highly skilled IT workers and leaders, professional service providers, consultants, and local training personnel when necessary.

Smart Cards

Cards allow clients to make small transactions in remote locations on an as-needed basis. Research shows that when people take out exactly the amount of money they need, they take smaller amounts and will save more. When sound microfinance providers are not available, people go to local money lenders for small transactions at inflated prices.

Credit and debit card services require either an ATM or an electronic point-of-service device for clients to perform various transactions, but the device must be online for it to work. Smart cards, however, operate as electronic passbooks. They have within them an embedded integrated-circuit chip, which can connect to a smart card reader either with direct physical contact or by remote radio frequency interfaces. All the transaction information is stored on one card, and in areas with unreliable communications they offer real advantages for people who live far from banking facilities. They allow for fingerprint scans for improved security.

Mobile Phone Banking

Because mobile phones are accessible virtually everywhere (and in fact they are often the only means of communication), they provide easy access to banking. Even people living in mud huts use cell phones to pay their bills and check current prices of grain, fish, and vegetables. China, for instance, already has the same number of mobile phones as all of Europe. According to *The Economist*,[8] India's telecom regulator reports that half of all urban dwellers have mobile or fixed phone subscriptions and the number grows by 8 million per month! Clients mainly use *short message service* (SMS) technology (limited to 160 text characters) to transfer and withdraw funds, to buy minutes for use on mobile phones, and to pay bills. Mobile phones have become "mobile wallets." In Uganda, for instance, mobile phone users exceed Internet users by a factor of ten. In the Philippines, Smart Money and Globe Cash are services offered by the top telecommunications providers to implement financial services via mobile phone.

MONEY IN A PHONE[9]

In Swahili, the word for "money" is *pesa*. In March 2007, Kenya, with funding from the Bill and Melinda Gates Foundation and others, introduced M-Pesa: mobile money. According to *Business Daily Africa*, six million users are now registered to use their mobile phones to move money around via person-to-person transfers. Tanzania is also using this system now, but with less dramatic results.

Safariphone teamed up with Vodafone to offer either a prepay or postpay system for clients who have a SIM card and a handset. There is free registration with an ID and they are set up with a personal identification number (PIN) and a secret security word. Clients must first go to a registered agent outlet to deposit money into the account and they get e-money in return. People can buy phone time, pay bills, check their balances, call for support, and choose any language offered. They can send money to another account, or withdraw money from any M-Pesa agent or participating ATM by signing a logbook in a store or franchise location to confirm the transaction.

Vodafone has recently partnered with Western Union and is facilitating money transfers from the United Kingdom to Kenya.

The service is very affordable but the early adopters were young, male, urban migrants, better educated and with higher incomes than the average population. Therefore, the service is used mainly in urban areas. However, it is in the rural areas that the providers are now focusing. Cash flow for the agents in remote locations is often a problem since more rural people withdraw cash than deposit. Until the banks increase the cash flow to those areas, agents will have a hard time getting to central banks to get the cash with which to operate. They often have to bike (since even shared taxis are very expensive) for hours to get to and from the urban banks. As a result, the closer the agent is to the bank, the more money he or she is able to "float." E-transactions, of course, would mitigate the money float issues as m-commerce becomes more common and more available.

Smartphones and Smart Entrepreneurs

When will mobile services in emerging markets evolve beyond the text messaging technology? This is the question raised by two young men who have created Frogtek, a for-profit social venture that "hatched" at Columbia Business School's MBA program, "leaped" to Colombia, and continued to grow across all of Latin America.[10]

They were inspired by a similar project by Women's World Banking. Frogtek clients wanted a "little gadget that the shopkeepers could use to understand their business operations better."[11] By partnering with a prominent Colombian NGO, David del Ser and Mark Pedersen initially are testing Frogtek's "little gadget" with 50 shopkeepers.

Smartphones such as BlackBerries, iPhones, and G1s function like a computer and can download new software applications. These phones have already transformed the way consumers in developed markets use and access data. (In fact, iPhone customers have, at this writing, downloaded a billion applications.)

So, it's only logical to assume that this technology will soon find its way into emerging markets as well. At least, that's what Frogtek is betting on. It has received initial investment funds to set up an office in Bogotá.

"A fundamental problem is finding a way to introduce advanced technological features to computer-illiterate customers in a way they can feel comfortable with. . . . We're inching toward creating a bunch of videos that explain how to use the mobiles, in lieu of a paper manual," said del Ser.[12]

Smartphone prices will have to come down and software will have to be developed to specifically service clients in developing countries for ventures such as Frogtek to truly take off to service the microretailers, the *tenderos* or neighborhood shopkeepers.

"Most of these Mom-and-Pop shops do not keep sales records, which can result in inefficient business operations and even bankruptcy. Hence, our first product is an accounting and inventory management tool that allows a shopkeeper to use a smartphone as a point-of-sale device; the camera even doubles as a bar code reader," according to del Ser.[13]

Smartphones generate basic reports about sales, inventory, and profitability, and information is also uploaded to Frogtek servers wirelessly for secure storage and further analysis. The data is safe in case the phones are lost, broken, or stolen. Frogtek figures they can improve shopkeepers' profitability by 25 percent as they move from painstakingly handwritten ledgers to online computing.

Frogtek believes it has the potential of reaching a half-million small shops in Mexico—the ones where families shop once or twice a day—and later to expand the offer to many more shops around the country. If its prototyping is successful, Frogtek plans to introduce additional products such as microinsurance and branchless banking.

"The *tenderos* are a fundamental pillar of their societies, since they provide the very basics needed to feed the base of the pyramid. Beyond that, they also help countless families by extending informal credit, which can make the difference between going hungry or eating when incomes are uncertain."[14]

Connecting Capital with People Who Need It

Capital is often lacking in poorer parts of the world, where it is needed most. Companies are exploring connecting lenders and borrowers in different parts of the world using web-based tools. These transactions can be riskier due to a lack of shared context and

KIVA: THE BIRTH OF PERSON-TO-PERSON FINANCE[15]

Kiva was started in 2005 by Matt and Jessica Flannery. It is an online lending platform that allows individuals in the developed world to loan to small business people in the developing world. Kiva operates in the microfinance space and works with a growing network of microfinance institutions (MFIs). The MFI partners post the profiles of their loan application to the Kiva website. Internet users in the

(continued)

United States, Canada, Europe, and beyond make small loans to these businesses. The businesses pay the lenders back over a period of about a year. Since inception, Kiva lenders have funded over $133 million in loans, with over 704,000 users in 196 countries.

Child Sponsorship Becomes Business Sponsorship

Matt and Jessica Flannery were living in San Francisco when they dreamed up the idea of loaning money to small businesses in developing countries via an online lending tool. Matt was a programmer at a high-tech firm and Jessica was working for a nonprofit that helped start small businesses in East Africa through small grants and loans. Matt and Jessica had grown up sponsoring children in Africa through church and families and had a keen interest in helping people in developing countries, but wanted to move away from helping via a benefactor–recipient relationship. Through numerous conversations, the idea emerged to extend the same sponsorship idea to businesses, rather than to families. Instead of grants, they could provide loans. Instead of a benefactor–recipient relationship, they could explore business partnership relationships. And they would create these connections though an online lending platform that would make the information flows between the lenders and borrowers easy, affordable, and accessible.

Creating a Bridge

There has been a growing group of investment funds that link the microfinance industry to the capital markets. These funds are growing, but are risk averse, so they want to lend only to MFIs that are large, well run, and can prove it through transparent financial statements. Kiva, however, is in a position to help MFIs because it has a risk-tolerant source of funds (individuals contributing small amounts at a time), and because it uses the Internet as a reputation-building mechanism. Through Kiva, MFIs build a track record for borrowing and paying back in real time. Users can monitor the performers of the MFI and the borrowers associated with it. Thus they are giving organizations the opportunity to prove themselves in a forum that will track, record, and highlight their achievements.

knowledge. Kiva, a U.S.-based company, is trying a novel approach to match lenders and borrowers and to reduce the risk of bad loans. Kiva lets U.S. residents loan small amounts of money to people in Asia and Africa through its website. Kiva sends its representatives into the field with a camera-equipped cell phone, which enables them to take pictures of borrowers and note their needs. Eventually they upload this information from their cell phone for the world to see the needs of a particular person and lend money to that borrower via Kiva's PayPal service in, for example, Kasur, Pakistan. Several lenders in the United States each contribute a fraction of the requested amount, therefore reducing each lender's risk. Kiva also follows up to document how the loan is being used.

Franchise Models

Microfinance providers can use existing franchises such as stores, post offices, or kiosks to perform basic banking transactions on behalf of the microfinance provider. These local locations usually have electricity, connectivity, and someone with computer skills, and are staffed by people whom the locals know and trust. Using existing venues for banking transactions reduces physical costs and meets people where they tend to go anyway, thus reducing their transportation costs. A merchant, for instance, can offer withdrawals, deposits, or payments to clients from some bank. That bank performs the requisite transaction through the merchant's account. The merchant charges a fee and cost-sharing plans vary, but the client ultimately benefits from the convenience, as do the microfinance institutions, which never have to open a branch office. While this is not a technical solution per se, ICT can make it easier to set up and manage such franchises.

MANAGEMENT INFORMATION SYSTEMS NOW AT THE CORE OF MICROFINANCE

Managing risk effectively is important to make microfinance profitable and hence sustainable. This means that one has to be able to gather and analyze accurate, timely, and high-quality information about customers and transactions. MIS technology, as exemplified in the SKS story, helps microfinance institutions track, analyze, and report on their operation. Small operations may manage with manual ledgers or spreadsheets, but it takes commercially designed software to track financial transactions and create reports for management donors and regulators. Scoring software can analyze data and predict customer behavior. Hand-held computers often record client information, and connectivity technologies, such as broadband or VSAT (very-small-aperture terminal), a wireless data connection via satellite, transmit data among staff and branches.

The use of information and communication technology by microfinance institutions is growing rapidly. For example, MIFOS, an initiative of the Grameen Foundation, offers financial software for the microfinance industry. Some projects that use the software are closely aligned with the Grameen Foundation, but many others are independent community efforts.

We know that having access to ICTs and ready information, for instance, about the weather, improvements in crop technology, and access to market prices, helps small farmers in developing countries to make better business decisions. The real power of information and communication technologies extends the reach of microfinance, and makes it more sustainable, affordable, and accessible. The Consultative Group to Assist the Poor (CGAP) sums up the benefits, saying it allows for:

- **More informed decisions.** A management information system that produces timely, accurate data about performance of financial services enables managers to continually evaluate performance, better predict cash needs, and anticipate and respond to crises rapidly. By upgrading its management information systems, Spandana (India) management was able to compile timely, reliable data and monitor performance across the microfinance institution's 45-branch network.
- **Increased flexibility.** Cooperativa 23 de Julio (Ecuador) transmits data instantaneously throughout its branch network using dial-up and satellite connections, which are faster and

cheaper than physically transferring data, and allows customers to bank at any branch.

- **Lower operating costs.** Mibanco (Peru) reduced loan origination costs (the costs required by the institution to produce the loan for the client) by 10 percent by streamlining its loan approval process with a scorecard to predict client repayment behavior.
- **Better reporting.** First Microfinance Bank (Pakistan) developed an MIS system that allows managers to produce reliable, standardized reports that follow accounting industry and national standards.
- **Increased deposits.** By placing easy-to-use ATMs in well-trafficked areas, Prodem (Bolivia) gave its clients the ability to save more often, and in smaller amounts, when they had cash available.
- **Improved customer convenience.** Cerudeb (Uganda) is experimenting with point-of-sale (POS) devices that enable clients to use their bank cards to withdraw cash at local retail outlets, instead of waiting in line at the branch.
- **More rural customers.** Standard Bank's (South Africa) low-minimum-balance, easy-to-use "ePlan" account can be opened at manned ATMs in rural areas where it would be too expensive to open branches.[16]

Without sound information systems, financial reporting and portfolio creation is nearly impossible. Financial statements, cash flow, and summary reports depend on that software to function properly. Institutions must be able to monitor, track, and report on performance in order to attract loan capital or grants intended for specific social purposes.

A number of off-the-shelf software applications exist for the basic financial reporting that MFIs require. However, high-volume transactions, group-solidarity lending, and field operations in poor rural locations create challenges and are difficult to support with commercial, traditional portfolio-management and accounting products. A robust software infrastructure will allow for better forecasting and planning by financial services providers, thereby improving their ability to manage funds, sustain their services, and maintain accountability to clients and investors.

WHERE DOES MICROFINANCE GO FROM HERE?

Microfinance is no longer a niche activity; it is becoming mainstream in global finance. Governments are stepping in to regulate it like other banking activities. These regulations will have their pros and cons. In reducing the variability and fraud they might at the same time dampen innovative experimentation. Organizations such as CGAP have begun to act as clearinghouses of best practices.

CONSULTATIVE GROUP TO ASSIST THE POOR

In their own words,

> CGAP is an independent policy and research center dedicated to advancing financial access for the world's poor. It is supported by over 30 development agencies and private foundations who share a common mission to alleviate poverty. Housed at the World Bank, CGAP provides market intelligence, promotes standards, develops innovative solutions, and offers advisory services to governments, microfinance providers, donors, and investors.[17]

CGAP has five core areas of work to help make their vision of permanent access to affordable and client-responsive financial services a reality.

1. Developing and strengthening a wide range of institutions and means, both financial and nonfinancial, that deliver financial services to the poor
2. Improving the quality and availability of information about institutional financial performance
3. Establishing supportive legal and regulatory frameworks
4. Improving aid effectiveness
5. Reaching poor and unserved clients and ensuring impact on their lives[18]

The Microfinance Gateway (www.microfinancegateway.org), a project of CGAP, is a comprehensive online resource for the global microfinance community. It includes research and publications, original articles, and organization and consultant profiles, as well as microfinance-related news items, announcements, events, and job opportunities.

Information available through the Microfinance Gateway is submitted by microfinance professionals or collected through staff research and is primarily in English.

The sector is also beginning to get coverage from market research companies such as Gartner. It is attracting bigger banks that see this sector as the next growth opportunity, even though the data on profitability and sustainability of the business models is still lacking. Most MFIs rely on simple ICTs today in order to reach the largest customer base with minimal costs. However, technical innovations such as Near Field Communication (NFC) chips embedded in cell phones will allow simple, low-cost, and secure two-way interactions between phones and POS terminals and so on. This could further improve access to banking for the poor and also improve banking for those in the developed world.

OPORTUNIDADES

The Bill and Melinda Gates foundation highlights one microfinance system that is making an impact in Mexico.

A recent pilot program is exploring ways to make vital, affordable financial services available to Mexico's rural poor at a place much closer to home: their local convenience store. Diconsa, a Mexican government agency, manages a network of more than 22,000 community-owned stores that sell food and other necessities in remote areas where some of the poorest Mexicans live. Diconsa believes the stores could also serve as a powerful platform to deliver social welfare payments and savings accounts to rural poor people.

To test its idea, the Mexican government, supported by the Bill and Melinda Gates Foundation's Financial Services for the Poor initiative, launched a pilot program in November 2008 to deliver government cash benefits, primarily Oportunidades payments, through Diconsa stores. Oportunidades payments are collected by an estimated 5 million poor Mexican citizens—including 60 percent of rural families—at distribution centers located mostly in urban areas. While this is usually easier for those living in cities, beneficiaries in remote areas are often required to travel long distances to collect their cash payments. For many, it is a costly journey that lasts a full day.

According to surveys, beneficiaries—typically women collecting payments on behalf of their families—reported that the new payment system saves them, on average, three to six hours of travel and $3 in travel costs. Diconsa store owners benefited from valuable training to teach them how to operate the payment system. They also noted increased sales because of the added foot traffic to their stores by beneficiaries . . . The aim is to expand the program to let an estimated 3 million rural families collect their benefits payments at Diconsa stores.[19]

Microfinance is not without its critics. Some have argued that the transaction costs are still too high and that the interest rates charged are exorbitant. Some of the ICT-based solutions outlined earlier may bring these costs down and potentially make the rates more affordable. Others have argued that the total number of people touched by microfinance is still very small compared to the scale of poverty at a global level. Worldwide, 3,133 microcredit institutions provided loans to 113.3 million clients, according to the *State of the Microcredit Summit Campaign Report 2006*. Unless the systems scale a lot more, their impact would be limited. Good data on the economic impact of microcredit is also difficult to come by. Critics have advocated alternatives such as equity investment instead of debt to stimulate entrepreneurship among the poor, or job creation programs instead.

CHALLENGES

Technology has the potential to have a significant impact on the access, quality, and affordability of financial services for the poor, but to date it has not yet had that impact. Efficient deployment of technology remains an elusive goal and there are very few examples of technology optimization at the institutional or sector level. Profound changes need to be created in order to realize universal advancement in technology for microfinance.

Evidence to support this point is found in the *Microfinance Banana Skins 2008 Report* written by the Center for the Study of Financial Innovation (CSFI), which was sponsored by CGAP and Citi. In this report, CSFI identified the biggest risks to the microfinance industry. Among the top ten largest risks were management quality (1), staffing (5), and managing technology (8). All of these problems can begin to be addressed by improving capacity building and training for MFI management and staff around proper technology use. It was acknowledged that managing new technology properly is the key element to ensuring better operations of the MFI.

Further exacerbating the problem of poor technology management at MFIs is the lack of reliable local technology service providers, which are often skeptical about the potential of the market. These providers are a fragmented group of individuals and companies servicing the technology needs of the microfinance sector, but they have largely been donor funded and have not been driven to invest in building their own capacity or to undertake the market building that is required. Furthermore, the aptitude required to manage enterprise-level software and the skills available in the markets where MFIs operate do not match. It is critical that there is stimulated demand from MFIs for IT services that inspire local businesses and build up the skills and resources required to deliver viable technology options for MFIs.

One thing that will not likely change is that a successful enterprise in this space will still require a creative set of public–private partnerships between telecommunications companies, banks, governments, NGOs, and entrepreneurs. We believe that one of the big open questions is whether an MFI like M-Pesa will grow to challenge commercial banks or companies such as Western Union on their own turf. If it does, then it would be yet another example of market disruption caused by a player that got its start in an emerging market.

SUMMARY POINTS

- Access to microcredit and basic affordable banking services can be a critical component of breaking the cycle of poverty.
- Extending credit to the poor requires reduced transaction costs, tools for assessing risk in the absence of purchasing power and asset base, and a business model that works with low-value transactions.
- Mobile phones, smart cards, and Internet-based systems are helping reduce transaction costs, matching capital to where it is most needed and providing access to small amounts of needed capital for the poor and underserved segments.

- Microfinance institutions are going mainstream and at the same time traditional banks are entering the arena to seek growth even though the business models are uncertain.
- Despite early successes with institutions like the Grameen Bank and M-Pesa, the number of people reached by microfinance is still small. Further reductions in transaction costs and innovations in both technologies and business models will be needed to scale up the reach and impact.
- As microfinance begins to be regulated, success requires even more of the right partnerships with governments, NGOs, telecommunications companies, and local entrepreneurs.

NOTES

1. The World Bank, "Microfinance: At a Glance," http://web.worldbank .org/WBSITE/EXTERNAL/NEWS/0,,contentMDK:20433592 ~menuPK:34480~pagePK:64257043~piPK:437376~theSitePK: 4607,00.html (accessed March 2, 2010).
2. CGAP, "Financial Access 2009: Measuring Access to Financial Services around the World," October 2009.
3. The World Bank, "Microfinance: At a Glance."
4. CGAP, "Financial Access 2009: Measuring Access to Financial Services around the World."
5. Subhash Bhatnagar, A. Dewan, M. M. Torres, and P. Kanungo, "Grameen Telecom: The Village Phone Program," www.w3.org/ 2008/02/MS4D_WS/papers/Mobile_phone_or_telecenter.pdf; Nevin Cohen, "What Works: Grameen Telecom's Village Phones," www .wri.org/publication/what-works-grameen-telecoms-village-phones, 2001; Grameen Foundation, www.grameenfoundation.org.
6. Allen L. Hammond, William J. Kramer, Robert S. Katz, Julia T. Tran, and Courtland Walker, *The Next 4 Billion: Market Size and Business Strategy at the Base of the Pyramid* (World Resources Institute and International Finance Corporation/World Bank Group, 2007); SKS India, www.sksindia.com; Tapan S. Parikh, "Rural Microfinance Service Delivery: Gaps, Inefficiencies and Emerging Solutions," International Conference on Information and Communication Technologies and Development, 2006, pp. 223–232, May 2006.
7. ICICI Bank, www.icicibank.com.
8. "Of Internet Cafes and Power Cuts," *The Economist*, February 7, 2008.

9. Nick Hughes and Susie Lonie, "M-Pesa: Mobile Money for the 'Unbanked': Turning Cell Phones into 24-Hour Tellers in Kenya," *Innovations*, Winter/Spring, 2007.

10. Mark Pedersen and David del Ser, "Smartphones and Emerging Markets: A New Technology Revolution?" Columbia Business School Public Offering, June 17, 2009.

11. Liz Matthews, "Can Technology Better the Lives of the Poor?" *Good Stories*, http://goodstories.wordpress.com/2009/07/15/can-technology-better-the-lives-of-the-poor, July 15, 2009.

12. Ibid.

13. Pedersen and del Ser, "Smartphones and Emerging Markets: A New Technology Revolution?"

14. Matthews, "Can Technology Better the Lives of the Poor?"

15. Matt Flannery, "Kiva and the Birth of Person-to-Person Microfinance," *Innovations* 2(1-2), Winter/Spring 2007.

16. Gautam Ivatury and Niole Pasricha, "Helping to Improve Donor Effectiveness in Microfinance," Consultative Group for the Poor (CGAP), Donor Brief Number 23, April 2005.

17. CGAP, "Who We Are," www.cgap.org/p/site/c/aboutus, 2010.

18. Zoran Stanisljevic, "Microcapital Story: CGAP and WIZZIT Collaborate to Expand Mobile Technology Services to Provide Branchless Banking to Poor Citizens in Rural South Africa," Microcapital.org, April 8, 2009.

19. Bill and Melinda Gates Foundation, "Diconsa: Bringing Financial Services to the Rural Poor in Mexico," www.gatesfoundation.org/grantee-profiles/Pages/diconsa-financial-services-for-the-rural-poor.aspx (accessed July 26, 2010).

CHAPTER 5

SUPPORTING THE WORLD IN A CHANGING ENVIRONMENT

WORLD OF LIMITED RESOURCES

If we continue with business as usual, by the early 2030s we will need two planets to keep up with humanity's demand for goods and services.
　　　　　　—Living Planet Report, World Wildlife Fund, 2008

The facts are sobering. Most of the world's arable land is already under cultivation. Much is lost to erosion or development every year. Water, the lifeblood of agriculture, is becoming a limited resource. Changing climate and weather patterns are rendering even the fertile areas vulnerable. Biodiversity is threatened around the world and its impact on the global food supply is not well understood. Yet, the demands on agriculture by a growing population continue to increase.

According to the World Wildlife Fund's 2008 *Living Planet* report, "humanity's demand on the planet has more than doubled over the past 45 years as a result of population growth and increasing individual consumption. In 1961, almost all countries in the world had more than enough capacity to meet their own demand; by 2005, the situation had changed radically, with many countries able to meet their needs only by importing resources from other nations."[1] Biodiversity is threatened by habitat loss, overexploitation of species, pollution, and climate change.

Vulnerability to Natural Disasters

Earthquakes, tsunamis, avalanches, hurricanes, and similar natural disasters have always been with us. Now, flooding, landslides, and serious environmental destruction accelerated by climate change have been added to that list. These events have the largest negative impact on people who are more likely to live on marginal landscapes and as such have the fewest resources to cope with it. The need to provide support when disaster strikes will rise as the full impact of climate change plays out in the coming decades.

The techno-optimists express confidence that the miracles of biotechnologies will create a second green revolution that will feed the world and avert mass famines and disasters. That may well happen, but it will take time. Is there a more near-term way to avert or delay the worst consequences of these trends? Is there a way to use resources more efficiently, to exploit local knowledge better, and to cut waste by making markets work better? Is it possible to get more accurate and timely information about the disappearance of forest cover, or the quality of air, or the availability of potable water to make better decisions? And when natural disasters strike, is there a way to minimize damage among the population that is the most vulnerable? Are information and communication technologies (ICTs) a part of the answer? These are some of the questions explored in this chapter.

MOVING SCIENCE FROM LABS TO THE FIELD

In the traditional worldview, scientists make discoveries in their labs, and these discoveries get turned into products and technologies, which in turn help solve critical problems, improve productivity, and such. In a world where the most pessimistic predictions on climate change are proving to be too conservative, that model will not work. We need a tighter connection between the scientists and those who are involved in agriculture and managing resources such as water, forests, and biodiversity. This means that science has to move beyond the confines of universities to farmers and forestry workers out tilling the land and managing forests. This is necessary to make better decisions about resources, and ICT can be instrumental in that transition.

Impact of ICT: Green Revolution 2.0?

ICT has been used in industrialized countries for years to aid agricultural production in what is referred to as *precision agriculture.*[2] The pervasiveness of computing, Internet, and satellite imaging technologies has allowed farmers to cut costs, improve yields, and get better prices by finding the right markets. For example, imagine a farmer who at the push of a button turns on a Global Positioning System (GPS) monitor on his tractor to pinpoint his exact location. Touching another button, the farmer can then display a series of Global Information System (GIS) maps to show where the soil is moist or eroded and where there are factors within the soil that limit crop growth. Next, the farmer can upload remote sensing data to show where the budding new crop is thriving (or not!) and then send results to an onboard machine that automatically regulates the application of fertilizer and pesticides. The U.S. Department of Agriculture, NASA, and the National Oceanic and Atmospheric Administration (NOAA) are among key agencies contributing to this revolution in large-scale agriculture.[3] The goal of this kind of innovation in ICT is aimed at improving farmers' profits and harvest yields while reducing the negative impacts on the environment that are caused by farms' overapplication of chemicals.

In developing countries, ICTs for agriculture are far less prevalent, however, primarily due to cost and infrastructure challenges. When in use, however, these tools can provide market information and troubleshooting and planting advice and even enhance agricultural productivity. Due to constraints, much ICT innovation in this space aims at both lowering costs and overcoming infrastructure challenges.

ICT Infrastructure in Rural and Underserved Communities

An information kiosk with PCs connected to the Internet and managed by a local agent or entrepreneur is the most prevalent example of providing access to relevant information to remote areas at a low cost. In general, kiosks are typically run as a partnership—for example, between a nongovernmental organization (NGO), a private company, and a government. About one-fourth of the services provided at the kiosk are related to agriculture, ranging from the sharing of best practices to prices, land records, and educational information, but also government services and other offerings as kiosk models have proliferated.[4]

Although significant investments have been made in these kiosks, their success and sustainability varies. Finding local expertise to run and maintain these kiosks can be a challenge. Their usefulness and success depends in large part on the operator, the relevance to the community, and their sense of ownership. PCs and Internet access costs are also considerable, and often prohibitive in these communities. Most of these programs survive through subsidies, so if the subsidies run out, the kiosks fall into disarray. The electricity infrastructure is unreliable and alternative energy sources add to the cost of running them. In the early days, not much content had been modified appropriately to be useful or relevant for the target audience. They tend to be used less by women or the uneducated population. Nonetheless, they represent an important step in reducing many of the "transaction costs" related to discovering and using the right information. They have also been successful in providing more convenient and transparent access to a variety of government resources.

Over the years, projects have taught us much about what works and doesn't work in extending information reach through ICT. Gyandoot (meaning "purveyor of knowledge") was a local government-run initiative in the state of Madhya Pradesh, India, where 40 percent of the population lived below the poverty line when the project started in 2000.[5] Educated kiosk operators were trained by local councils to run the centers as entrepreneurs. Drishtree, the parent organization of Gyandoot, continues to show success based on this entrepreneurial model with investment from supporters such as the Acumen Fund, a premier social venture group.[6] Another project in India, iKisan, required farmers to become members to benefit from services while its operators, agriculture college graduates, acted as important interfaces between them and the computers.[7] In this way, operators are able to advise farmers on diseases and pests and even offer offline services such as crop diagnostics, disease and pest management, soil testing, sampling, and fertility.

The arrival of mobile phones marked the next stage in the evolution of PC-based information centers. Warana Wired, a project associated with an Indian NGO sugar cooperative, used a management information system to enable speedy and accurate data exchanges between the sugar factory and farmers—and was an early adopter of GIS maps in the local language to reach out to more of the local population. When the project encountered PC problems ranging from rugged rural conditions and rising maintenance costs to problems with power, researchers decided to replace the PCs with short message service (SMS)–enabled phones. This updated system—Warana Unwired—is truly mobile and available 24 hours. SMS Sokoni represents a similar example in Kenya.

Many other organizations around the world have used mixed techniques to disseminate information to farmers. In Egypt, VERCON (Virtual Extension and Research Community Network) offers a web-based portal system to exchange critical information.

SMS SOKONI

SMS Sokoni in Kenya empowers farmers through an SMS market price service. In partnership with African mobile service provider Safaricom Limited, the Kenya Agricultural Commodity Exchange (KACE), a private-sector firm started in 1997, started SMS Sokoni to facilitate linkages between sellers and buyers of agricultural communities by providing relevant and timely marketing information and intelligence.

SMS Sokoni has several market information points from which it receives its information. Information kiosks are located near where agricultural commodity buyers and sellers meet to provide low-cost access to farmers. KACE workers collect information on prices from these kiosks and then send it to the farmers, buyers, and exporters through SMS. A client is charged 7 shillings for each final market price that is requested by the client.

According to Mobile Active.org, "although the entry costs and per-unit costs for a KACE user are low, farmers need to feel that they get value for their fees to sign up and for the service to be sustainable in the longer term." Farmers have tripled their earnings due to their access to information about potential buyers and prices. The organization further argues that the "partnership with a mobile service provider has given SMS Sokoni a wider reach and has helped reduce costs, which largely explains why it is popular. Charging user fees may ensure sustainability after the donor phase."[8]

FoodNet in Uganda is a national system to disseminate agricultural market price information via newspaper, Internet, radio, and SMS on mobile phones. Others have used a cell phone–based infrastructure, or so-called *M-vironment framework*.[9] An M-vironment framework uses two kinds of ICTs: mobile phones and radios. The mobile phone text messaging service is used to provide market prices to farmers, employment vacancy alerts to unemployed, and local news to disadvantaged communities and slum dwellers. The Worldspace satellite radio receivers are used to disseminate locally relevant content in audio and data formats to pastoralists in arid areas.

There is growing interest among students and developers to make an impact and contribute through technology to face environmental challenges of our times. For example, since its beginning in 2003, Microsoft's Imagine Cup is a global competition focused on finding solutions to global issues. Open to students around the world, the Imagine Cup provides a serious challenge with a contest that spans a year, beginning with local, regional, and online contests whose winners go on to attend the Worldwide Finals held in a different location every year. The intensity of the work brings students together, and motivates the competitors to give it their all. Although solutions span sectors and technologies, many concentrate

---

SMART OPERATIONAL AGRICULTURE KIT

Climate change has meant that farmers are seeing water become scarcer, which is affecting their farming yields. A student team from four different universities in Australia created SOAK to address one of the most important issues currently facing the world.

2007 saw Australian farmers having the worst crop production in 20 years, with a 59 percent reduction from the previous year. Of the world's population, 12.6 percent currently suffer from malnutrition; therefore, supporting farmers in increasing their crop yields will not only be of benefit to the farmers, it will have a further effect of enlarging the available food supply to the world population.

SOAK addresses the problem of limited water supplies by empowering the farmers to make decisions which affect water usage on their farm. Environmental sensors and weather forecasts are used to determine when watering their crops would be optimal. By implementing agriculture best practices, farmers can specify what conditions must be met before SOAK will water their plants. An example is the farmer configuring the system to water grapes weekly during the initial growth stages, but after the grape vine has grown fruit, restricting the water supply so as to drive up the sugar content (and sweetness).

Farmers can be notified of a field reaching a critical moisture level via SMS or "Microsoft Live Alerts." This could be extended to notify them of a critical failure on the farm such as a water line bursting. The principal differentiator for SOAK over current market offerings is the cheaper cost to install a SOAK implementation on a farm. Standard server hardware and commercial off-the-shelf sensor hardware can be easily integrated into the system, bringing the entry requirements down within reach of most farmers.[10]

on overcoming barriers stemming from environmental challenges, such as Smart Operational Agriculture Kit (SOAK).

Improved Resource Management

As resources become scarce and expensive, it will become critical to manage them efficiently and to use them in an optimal manner. Water needs to be directed where it is most beneficial. Waste needs to be minimized. Crops need to be grown on land that is the most suited to it. And market-based approaches may become necessary to do resource distribution. In order to work well, markets require high-quality, reliable information.

One community in Musingini, Kenya, is working with Safaricom and Grundfos Lieflink, a division of the Danish pump maker Grundfos Group, to implement a solar-powered, pay-for-use water-vending system using the M-Pesa backbone (see Chapter 4 for more information on M-Pesa). The solar-powered well is activated using a smart card, which permits water to flow until either the card is removed or the user's account runs out of credit. Villagers can use the M-Pesa system to add more credit to the smart card via their mobile phones. The system is being tested across Kenya, and by the end of the year at least 20 communities will be combining mobile banking and solar-powered wells.

The widespread availability of affordable sensor devices, combined with wireless technologies and new software programs, is enabling researchers in the earth and environmental sciences to collect and analyze large volumes of information that can dramatically improve our understanding of underlying environmental processes and develop more reliable models and prediction systems. In one bold experiment, Swiss scientists have put sensors on glaciers in the Alps that measure the progression of the glaciers and allow the scientists to calibrate the effect of climate change on water supply. These sensors rely on wireless sensor networks to communicate data to the base stations. Once this technology is perfected it could be deployed elsewhere and have a big impact since many of the rivers that feed the plains in India, China, and other populated countries rely on glacier melt.

Microsoft Research has collaborated with researchers around the world to develop sophisticated data management and visualization tools that make it easier for scientists to understand the huge volumes of information being collected in a range of fields, such as oceanography, astronomy, hydrology, climatology, and energy management. For instance, researchers are helping to develop tools for the FLUXNET project, a global network of scientists who are using micro-meteorological towers to measure the role that plant photosynthesis plays in removing carbon from the atmosphere.

In an international collaboration called the SWISS Experiment, scientists are using web-based tools developed by Microsoft researchers to view huge quantities of environmental data more efficiently and in richer detail than previous technologies allowed. Computer scientists at the Lawrence Berkeley National Laboratory have also teamed up with hydrologists at the University of California, Berkeley, to create "digital watersheds" that combine decades of hydrological data with more recent data from sensor networks. The team is developing software tools that enable scientists to analyze large-scale data sets in a fraction of the time it would previously have taken. Finally, Microsoft researchers are developing a new tool, SciScope, a web-based search engine designed specifically to locate meteorological, hydrological, and water- and soil-quality data from numerous data repositories and retrieve it in a consistent format. Still in its beta version, SciScope already provides access to data from about 9.5 million sensors across the United States, enabling users to access a broad range of environmental data—from precipitation, snow pack, and stream flow measurements to data on solar radiation, water quality, and biodiversity.

Despite innovations like these, we don't see many examples of innovative solutions scaling to meet emerging market needs. For example, LifeStraw, by European-based Vestergaard Frandsen, is an affordable point-of-use water filter aimed at getting clean water to more households, especially in the developing world.[11] Although the straw removes 99.9 percent of viruses, parasites, and bacteria that cause diarrhea, dysentery, typhoid, and even cholera, sales have been nominal. This begs the questions of many experiments: What keeps potentially revolutionary innovations from scaling? Are enterprises unable to find cost-effective models? Do they have trouble working directly with the intended audience?

Enhanced Local Knowledge

One reason that innovations don't scale to their potential is that often they are not necessarily designed with local context, microclimates, or other nuances in mind. For example, many countries have an extensive system of outreach to educate the farmers on the latest techniques and to help them grapple with the local problems of pestilence, crop yields, and such; all too often, however, information is not adapted to precise local conditions, nor is it mediated by a trusted member of the community. This makes information less likely to be used in practice. Digital Green tried to address this by enabling local farmers to solve local problems and to communicate the solutions to the rest of their community.

While fleet services and operators such as Federal Express in the United States can use precise weather forecasts to reduce their transportation costs and minimize weather-related disruption, farmers in developing regions often cannot afford to get targeted forecasts for their geographies. Regional weather forecasts are not fine-grained enough to help deal with microclimates and the impacted population is not seen as having enough purchasing power to afford these services. But new technologies have the power to change that.

Local climate change models can help regional planners take meaningful action to prepare their own communities for the impact of climate change. The research community is active in this space and new business opportunities are likely to follow suit.

Better Market Arbitrage

Market transactions in agriculture depend on information, but in many rural areas market information is lacking because of

DIGITAL GREEN: TRAINING FARMERS WITH LOCAL TALENT AND LOCAL KNOWLEDGE[12]

Digital Green (DG) is a research project that seeks to disseminate targeted agricultural information to small and marginal farmers in India through digital video. The Digital Green system sustains relevancy in a community by developing a framework for participatory learning. The system includes a digital video database, which is produced by farmers and experts. The content within this repository is of various types, and sequencing enables farmers to progressively become better farmers. Content is produced and distributed over a hub-and-spokes-based architecture in which farmers are motivated and trained by the recorded experiences of local peers and extension staff. In contrast to traditional extension systems, DG follows two important principles: (1) cost realism, essential for scaling the system up to a significant number of villages and farmers and (2) building systems that solve end-to-end agricultural issues with interactivity that develops relationships between people and content. The DG system provides structure to a traditional, informally trained vocation. The system improves the efficiency of extension programs by delivering targeted content to a wider audience and enabling farmers to better manage their farming operations with reduced field support.

Digital Green has demonstrated early success in the popularization of sustainable farming practices in the 12 villages in India in which the system is currently deployed. At least five times more farmers attempted better agricultural practices after integration of the DG system over the NGO's previous efforts. Today, DG is still in its early stages but aims to scale its system to offer relevant agricultural extension services to a much wider population of farmers.

the distance from the market. ICT can improve the efficiency of transactions between rural areas and core markets by decreasing the information asymmetry between the market and the farmers, which means that farmers can have the same information as the markets even though they are not there. There have been many technologies

AAQA: AN SMS-BASED HELPLINE FOR FARMERS WITH MICRO WEATHER FORECASTS

Agrocom, a spinoff from the Indian Institute of Technology (IIT) Mumbai, developed AAQA (Almost All Questions Answered) to provide farmers with much-needed information. The following report from the *Hindustan Times* shows how ICT can help:

On the evening of November 11, Nashik grape farmer Arun More's cell phone beeped with an SMS from a lab 220 km away at the Indian Institute of Technology (IIT), Mumbai. Sent by three-month-old Agrocom Pvt. Ltd., the text message predicted unseasonal rain two days later in his village of Pimpalgaon Basant.

And that's exactly what happened. "But since I had prior information, I could spray fungicide accordingly. I managed to save my orchard from the mildew that would have destroyed the crop," says More. Agrocom is the brainchild of a group of software engineers associated with IIT's Developmental Informatics Laboratory. In 2004, tying up with the state's Krishi Vigyan Kendra, it set up the online portal, Almost All Questions Answered, getting experts to answer farmer queries from all over Maharashtra, and now other states, usually within 24 hours.

"Our interaction with farmers suggested that there was a crying need for accurate and timely weather information. Agrocom wants to address that," says its marketing head, Shantanu Inamdar. And the SMS service did just that.

This is how it works: Farmers pay a small monthly charge, and receive SMSs every three days—more frequently if forecasts are grim—from Agrocom that predict cloud cover and rain. "In the next few months, we will formulate training programs on crop cultivation and poultry, mechanics, as well as rural health issues like dengue treatment," informs MD Anil Bahumani.[13]

(e.g., telephony, radio, and, computers) that have been tried in rural areas around the world to redress this asymmetry.

In Tumaco, Colombia, microwave radio telephone systems were installed in 1994; within three years of these systems being installed there were already much better market and trade operations. The example of SMS use by fishermen in Kerala in India is well documented. It showed that a simple SMS-based service made the market more efficient by allowing fishermen to bring their catch to where the demand was the highest, even though it didn't necessarily improve their incomes. The Grameen Phone, for example, not only allows the rural areas to be connected with the rest of the world but also provides livelihoods for a few women in the village. The reduced transaction costs of mobile phones make them especially attractive as a means of communication.

To enhance economic opportunities for China's migrant workers and rural learning, Microsoft China in 2004 initiated its Unlimited Potential Program. Working in partnerships with domestic and international NGOs, local governments, and community organizations, Microsoft donated cash, software, and curriculum to establish 15 Community Technology Learning Centers in nine provinces and cities in China.

A Connecticut businessman named Ed Bullard founded TechnoServe, or Technology in the Service of Mankind, in 1968. While volunteering at a hospital in rural Ghana, he was struck by how difficult it was for hardworking people in the area to lift themselves out of poverty. So he created an organization to transform lives by providing poor people access to productivity-enhancing tools and thus enable them to use technology to generate livelihoods. Today, TechnoServe focuses on developing entrepreneurs, building businesses and industries, and improving the business environment. Working with a range of public- and private-sector partners, such as the U.S. Agency for International Development, the Rockefeller, W.K. Kellogg, and Bill and Melinda Gates foundations, and Microsoft, TechnoServe implements a private-enterprise approach, including advancing technologies that serve farmers.

Data Collection by Citizen Scientists

Outbreaks of plant diseases, specific information on rainfall and weather conditions, precise crop yields, and the levels of pollutants or contaminants in soil, water, and air are just some of the parameters that the local population, properly equipped and trained, can gather much more effectively than scientists primarily based in their labs and universities. These in turn can help scientists

TECHNOSERVE COFFEE INITIATIVE

TechnoServe's fact sheet tells its story:

A grant of $47 million from the Bill and Melinda Gates Foundation to TechnoServe is helping small-scale farmers in East Africa boost their income by improving the quality of their coffee. In addition, Microsoft provided the organization with a software grant so they could develop their technology systems to undertake the projects. TechnoServe is partnering with approximately 180,000 farmers over four years to provide support in the areas of quality management and agronomy, offering farmers the potential to increase their incomes.

The Coffee Initiative is based on an approach that has proven successful in breaking the cycle of poverty for coffee farmers in Latin America and Africa, and builds on TechnoServe's four decades of experience working with coffee farmers. The project is currently being implemented in Ethiopia, Kenya, Rwanda, and Tanzania, and could expand into other countries in the future.

TechnoServe provides technical and business expertise to help small-scale farmers produce higher-quality coffee and secure price premiums in the marketplace. Specifically, TechnoServe works with selected small-scale farmers, whose farms enjoy the agroclimatic conditions required to produce coffee sought out by the world's most discerning buyers. Areas of training include quality coffee production and processing, business management, and quality coffee assessment.

TechnoServe starts by listening to its clients and other stakeholders in the coffee industry to understand concerns and constraints. TechnoServe business advisors work hand-in-hand with farmers while maintaining strong relationships with the local coffee industry. Historically, this approach has been successful in creating "win-win" outcomes for farmers, processors, and exporters.[14]

improve their models and adapt them to local conditions. One doesn't need many sophisticated tools to do that; a regular cell phone with appropriate software, the cell phone camera, and inexpensive sensors connected to the cell phone will suffice. To organize and analyze all such information collected is, of course, more challenging.

When the data being collected is about the water level in rivers, or asthma-inducing pollutants in air, it can be literally a matter of life and death. Such systems can be built at low cost using mobile technologies in vulnerable areas and can save lives. A team of researchers at the Massachusetts Institute of Technology (MIT) in Cambridge designed an affordable automated flood warning system that takes into account an array of challenges in the developing world: lack of resources and trained personnel, harsh physical conditions, large physical areas to monitor, and a partly illiterate population. The researchers relied on the memories of community members in the Aguan River region to chart recent floods and field-tested a prototype system in collaboration with Fundación San Alonso Rodríguez (FSAR), a Honduran nonprofit organization dedicated to providing communities with technical assistance in such areas as agriculture and sanitation. A wireless sensor network like this one can provide early flood detection for underserved communities and countries, especially where devastation caused by flooding is commonplace. Even more exciting is that future applications include agricultural field monitoring, hospital patient systems, traffic congestion relief systems, and certain types of natural disaster monitoring.

MINIMIZING THE IMPACT OF NATURAL DISASTERS

We learned from the 2004 Indian Ocean tsunami that a dollar spent in preparation for disasters goes much further than a dollar donated after the disaster. The goal of this unique public-private partnership is to strengthen emergency response missions by creating technology coordination, faster response times, and more lives saved.
— *Paul Margie, Senior Director of Technology Partnerships at the UN Foundation*

Through partnerships between businesses, leading NGOs, international humanitarian organizations, and government organizations, innovative technologies have been created to help make communities become more resilient in disaster prevention, preparedness, response, and recovery. The evolution of technologies used in disasters—natural or otherwise—is broad, from radios to mobile phones.

Back in 1999, Microsoft's disaster relief work began with a partnership with the United Nations High Commissioner for Refugees (UNHCR) in response to the increasing stream of refugees out of Kosovo. According to the website, "Microsoft mobilized 100 employee volunteers and developed a mobile registration kit that used technology to help 500,000 Kosovo refugees reestablish their identities. This helped reunite families, prove citizenship and property ownership, and provide access to health care and other services. Since then, Microsoft volunteers have improved the registration kits for use by UNHCR in many other parts of the world."[15] Efforts and technologies have evolved, as have the needs.

Dealing effectively with natural disasters requires managing the multitude of information coming from many different sources. After a natural disaster the relief team has to assess the number of people dead and number of people injured, and identify any health issues and food requirements for the living. They also have to assess the probability of recurrence such as aftershocks. They need to determine whether a given place is safe for people to be or whether the people need evacuation. High-quality information is needed to make these decisions and then to implement them. Sophisticated systems are required to help make these decisions. These tools help make sense of all the information floating around in the chaos after a disaster and enable relief agencies to allocate resources to the right place at the right time.

Disaster Alert Systems

Many developing countries do not have disaster alert systems in place, partly due to the lack of infrastructure to get this information to people in remote areas. After the Sumatra earthquake on December 26, 2004, which led to a tsunami that took the lives of over 230,000 people, there has been a movement to set disaster management and alert systems. Sahana was one such system that was built just weeks after the Sumatra earthquake by a group of volunteers from the Sri Lankan IT industry and spearheaded by the Lankan Software Foundation.[16] Over 40 volunteers from various groups contributed to the creation of Sahana. The system keeps track of relief organizations working in the disaster region, provides a repository where agencies can match the request of aid with pledges of support, and includes a registry of all shelters and camps and their services and a missing-persons log. This system has been deployed during earthquakes in other areas, including Pakistan and the Philippines. Collaborative mapping applications and mobile messaging are just a couple of additional services provided by the system.

Another example, Ushahidi, offers an innovative outsourcing disaster management tool. Although it was started in Kenya, the website has been instrumental in the recent earthquake in Haiti and worldwide.

Inventory Management Systems

While information regarding the disaster-hit area is necessary, it is also important to have information regarding where the relief could come from. Therefore, one needs an inventory of the available aid in

---

USHAHIDI[17]

Ushahidi means "testimony" in Swahili. The website was created after post-election violence in Kenya in 2008 to map incidents of violence. Over 45,000 users submitted reports via the Web and mobile phone at the time showing a need for such a platform. Since then, Ushahidi has worked "to create a platform that individuals or organizations can use to set up in their own way to collect and visualize information. The core platform it creates allows for plug-ins and extensions so that it can be customized for different locales and needs."

Because the Ushahidi Platform was built for information collection, visualization, and interactive mapping, it has been used to map incidents of xenophobic violence in South Africa, aid in peacekeeping efforts in the Democratic Republic of the Congo, and monitor election results in India. More recently, the platform was used to create Chile and Haiti "Crisis Maps" to track the post-earthquake crisis response and recovery efforts.

the areas closest to the affected areas. If this information is handy, it is possible to get these resources to the people very quickly. In India, the Ministry of Home Affairs has taken the lead on disaster management and mitigation. It has undertaken many ICT-based initiatives to help the disaster managers function efficiently.

The Indian government has prepared a database of these resources that can be managed at the district level. This inventory is called the India Disaster Resource Network (IDRN).[18] It can be accessed by key government officials, district-level personnel, corporate bodies, and public-sector units. In this database, entries are made both on a district and on a state level. The district authority is responsible for compiling and updating its inventory data to the central server with the help of district departments. A GIS-based database is used to decide the mobilization of the right resources to the right locations within the shortest response time. The ministry, with support from the United Nations Development Programme (UNDP), is in the process of developing GIS-based tools for emergency management on a pilot basis.

Information Networks at the Disaster Site

From the moment a disaster strikes and there is a loss of most traditional communication networks, one needs to manage all of the information that is used in the relief process at the disaster site. NetHope provides a summary of the lessons learned from ten disaster sites.

NETHOPE REPORT

One of NetHope's case study reports summarizes knowledge from disaster relief efforts in Afghanistan, Iraq, Liberia, Iran, Sudan, Guatemala, Indonesia, Sri Lanka, Pakistan and Lebanon. It divides the disaster into the following three stages:

Stage 1: Within hours of disaster striking. This is when the first relief workers arrive at the site. One of the first needs at this stage is to assess the damage and transmit pictures and information regarding the relief materiel and personnel required to the head offices. In such a situation one needs highly mobile computing and ICTs that can be temporary and transient.

Disaster	Country	Period	Stage	Agencies	NetHope Contribution
War	Afghanistan	2002	2 & 3	STC CARE MC	VSAT installation in Kabul and Talogan
War	Iraq	2003	2 & 3	STC CARE MC CRS WV	VSAT and LAN installations in six cities
War	Liberia	2003	2	CCF MC AA CRS Oxfam WV	Satellite/wireless connectivity in Monrovia
Earthquake	Iran	2004	1 & 2	AA Oxfam STC RI WV MC	RBGAN donation for deployment in Bam
War	Sudan	2004	3	WV Oxfam STC MC	VSAT acquisition
Hurricane	Guatemala	2005	1	CI CARE CCF	Connectivity investigation
Tsunami	Indonesia/ Sri Lanka	2005/6	1, 2, & 3	STC CRS Oxfam WV CCF IRC AA	VSAT RBGAN NRK deployment in 16 locations
Earthquake	Pakistan	2005	1, 2, & 3	AA CARE CRS IRC MC Oxfam STC WV	VSAT deployment in 14 locations
Earthquake	Indonesia	2006	1	Oxfam Plan WV AA STC CRS CCF	Connectivity investigation
War	Lebanon	2006	2 & 3	World Vision Oxfam CRS CCF Mercy Corps	Connectivity investigation (ongoing at time of writing)

Figure 5.1 NetHope Disaster Engagements

Source: Dipak Basu and William Brimley, "Disaster Relief," whitepaper, www.nethope.org/images/uploads/casestudies/DisasterRelief.pdf, September 26, 2006.

(continued)

Stage 2: Within two weeks of a disaster striking. Relief teams begin to arrive at the scene, as the risk of disease and malnutrition increases. At this stage one needs to be able to assess the needs of those affected by the disaster and then transmit that information to the right places. Along with the transmission of the demand for materials, relief supplies start flooding into the area and there is a need for a system that allocates these supplies first to the people that need them the most. In this kind of situation, relief agencies set up highly mobile offices. Therefore, there is a need for portable devices that can function with limited infrastructure.

Stage 3: From one month following a disaster to multiyear. Many agencies start providing long-term aid in rebuilding the area and continuous support to those affected, as well as other short- and long-term services such as counseling and family reunification. At this time the relief agencies often set up a more permanent office in the affected area that can have a bigger impact on the community. The ICTs required at this time are more long term than the transient, temporary ones available in stages 1 and 2.[19]

As the NetHope example shows, the initial stages of crisis prioritize the rescue and treatment of survivors and the communication between relief workers and the communities in need and of support. To assist with these, NetHope provides a "Network Relief Kit" (NRK) that individuals can carry to a disaster site to provide instant communication. The kits offer:

- Wireless local connectivity for both voice and data
- Voice communication via high-frequency radio to a telecom hub or data communication via Internet by satellite
- Optional reach up to 100 km (with booster/repeater)
- Internet access for voice and data
- Acceptable speed and quality
- Cost control capability

- Firewall capability to centrally restrict destination addresses
- Alternative sources of power (solar, car battery)

The NRK is an affordable tool that requires little to no technical expertise to install and operate. Another promising technology NetHope is testing is a portable network—Inmarsat's BGAN (Broadband Global Area Network)—which utilizes a secure 3G mobile service. Enabled by Inmarsat's satellite, BGAN offers simultaneous voice and data service, data transfer speeds up to 492 kbps, streaming service for live video or videoconferencing, standard or Bluetooth phone calling and text messaging. BGAN can also operate within challenging environments and under extreme temperatures. With the spread of satellite networks, 3G networks will be used a lot more in natural disaster situations to transfer data where there is a lack of infrastructure.

WHERE DO WE GO FROM HERE?

Use of ICT to help deal with a changing climate and environment is at an early stage compared to health care, microfinance, and education. There are promising research results as well as successful pilots but few sustainable businesses. The scarcity of resources is therefore even more acute. But the imperative keeps getting stronger with every Katrina, shrinking glacier, and loss of arable land and biodiversity.

It also means that funding from foundations and NGOs will continue to play a big role until viable business models emerge. The lack of infrastructure that hampers other initiatives is a factor in this field as well, but its effects are being mitigated by the rise of mobile phone–based infrastructure.

In the near term, there is an opportunity to take services such as hyperlocal weather and local water information that target rich farmers and resource managers in developed countries and make them available affordably on the mobile phone–based infrastructure in developing countries. The development of local climate models and the ability to tap local populations to collect precise environmental data in real time will improve scientists' ability to forecast and hopefully mitigate some of the worst effects of climate change.

SUMMARY POINTS

- Effective management of natural resources is becoming more critical in the presence of climate change and rapid degradation of air, water, and arable land.
- ICT is playing an important role in tracking, measuring, and analyzing a vast amount of relevant environmental data to help make better decisions.
- Science is of necessity moving out from the laboratories to the field, where the citizens who are closest to the problem are playing an important role in data collection and analysis.
- The ability to implement and develop local climate models with ICT may help minimize the worst effects of climate change.
- Disasters are inevitable, and the need for effective management of the aftermath will continue to increase. ICT plays a big role in preparing for them, dealing with the aftermath, and helping with the long-term recovery.

NOTES

1. World Wildlife Fund, *Living Planet* (Geneva, Switzerland: World Wildlife Fund, 2008).
2. Doug Rickman, J. C. Luvall, Joey Shaw, Paul Mask, David Kissel, and Dana Sullivan, "Precision Agriculture: Changing the Face of Farming," *GeoTimes*, November 2003.
3. David Herring, "Precision Farming, NASA Earth Observatory," http://earthobservatory.nasa.gov/Study/PrecisionFarming/precision_farming.html, January 29, 2001.
4. Jessica Rothenberg-Aalami and Joyojeet Pal, "Rural Telecenter Impact Assessments and the Political Economy of ICT for Development (ICT4D)," Berkeley Roundtable for the International Economy (BRIE) Working Paper 164, 2005.

5. Shaik N. Meera, Anita Jhamtani, and D.U.M. Rao, "Information and Communication Technology in Agricultural Development: A Comparative Analysis of Three Projects from India." Agricultural Research and Extension Network, Network Paper No. 135, January 2004.

6. Ibid.

7. Ibid.

8. Esther Nasikye, "Mobile Telephony Makes a Difference in Livelihoods," http://mobileactive.org/Mobile+Telephony+Makes+ a+Difference+in+Livelihoods (accessed March 2010). See also Anja Bangelstorff, "Use Your Mobile Phone for Marketing," *The Organic Farmer* 30, November 2007.

9. Wainaina Mungai, "Using ICTs for Poverty Reduction and Environmental Protection in Kenya: The 'M-vironment' Approach," in *A Developing Connection: Bridging the Policy Gap between the Information Society and Sustainable Development*, edited by Terri Willard and Maja Andjelkovic (International Institute for Sustainable Development, 2005) 43–85. www.iisd.org.

10. David Burela, "SOAK: Smart Operational Agriculture Kit," http://davidburela.files.wordpress.com/2008/05/soak-executive-summary.pdf, May 22, 2008.

11. Vestergaard Frandsen, "Lifestraw," www.vestergaard-frandsen.com/lifestraw (accessed July 27, 2010).

12. Digital Green, "Overview," http://research.microsoft.com/en-us/um/india/projects/digitalgreen/default.htm (accessed July 2008).

13. Chitrangada Choudhury, "From IIT Lab, Engineers SMS Help to Farmers," *Hindustan Times*, December 30, 2006. www.hindustantimes.com/StoryPage/Print/196823.aspx.

14. TechnoServe, "TechnoServe Coffee Initiative," www.technoserve.org/assets/documents/jan2009coffeeinitiativefactsheet.pdf (accessed October 2009).

15. Microsoft Corporation, "Global Partnerships," www.microsoft.com/about/corporatecitizenship, 2010.

16. Sahana, www.sahanafoundation.org (accessed July 27, 2010).

17. Ushahidi, "About Ushahidi," www.ushahidi.com/about (accessed March 3, 2010).

18. Indian Disaster Resource Network, www.idrn.gov.in (accessed July 27, 2010).

19. Dipak Basu and William Brimley, "Disaster Relief," whitepaper, www.nethope.org/images/uploads/casestudies/DisasterRelief.pdf, September 26, 2006.

CHAPTER 6

CONCLUSION

Harnessing Disruption

In the preceding chapters we have shown that technology, especially information and communication technologies (ICTs), conceived to meet the needs of those at the bottom of the economic pyramid can be disruptive to the status quo. When it is affordable, relevant, and accessible, technology can disrupt or displace existing norms. It can also enable a "leapfrogging" of sorts—allowing new players or business models to emerge that reach new constituencies and have an impact beyond those enabled by incumbent tools and business practices.

We have shown that technology can also be an amazing tool for social and economic development. It can help people get a better education and learn new skills to earn a living wage or start a business. By reducing transaction costs and by reducing the level of skills required to deliver services, it can broaden access to health care, banking, education, and environmental services. Though the pace of innovation in each of the sectors is not the same (sectors such as banking are further along than education, for example), their direction and momentum are quite clear.

We can already see the broad outlines of these technologies. These are primarily smart mobile devices connected to the Internet and all the powerful information resources and tools that reside in that cloud. They have democratized access to information and to computing itself. People and organizations around the world can access information and communicate and collaborate in new and potentially powerful ways. This new computing paradigm is touching all of our lives, but especially those of social innovators, nongovernmental organizations (NGOs), and corporations developing solutions that reach the underserved communities around the world. What we have shown is that technical and business model innovations are necessary and indeed critical if we are to achieve our boldest dreams of universal education and health care, a sustainable environment, and economic conditions that positively impact the poor.

We have also shown that realizing this bold dream will require engagement and partnerships between the private sector, governments, foundations, and development agencies, with social innovators and NGOs playing a key role in the implementation and distribution of innovative solutions.

We have also raised some fundamental issues.

REIMAGINING THE ROLE OF EXPERTS

What is the role of experts and specialists when technology is used to "de-skill" critical services to make them affordable and accessible? The need for experts doesn't go away; we will continue to need specialized doctors, educators, bankers, and scientists. In fact, their sphere of influence would be even greater than before since their impact would be multiplied by the less specialized local entrepreneurs who are connected with them through ICT. However, some of their more routine tasks will get encoded in scripts and procedures that the non-specialists can follow. Experts traditionally enjoyed their prominent role because of the rarity of their expertise and the cost of providing their expertise. But that also limited access to the masses. In the future, these experts will focus on branding and disseminating this expertise at scale through local entrepreneurs and refining their expertise by acquiring local knowledge through the same network. Sustainability would require coming up with ways to share in the value that is created by the combination of the experts and non-experts.

In health care this takes the form of equipping physician extenders and public health workers with powerful diagnostic tools and basic training so that they can provide basic services and triage for the communities they serve. They are still connected to the experts using the communication tools we have described in the book, to seek advice and help. However, the experts are tapped only when they are needed rather than for common and routine procedures and decisions. Their presence in the system is critical, however, since without them the system won't be able to function and provide the full range of care for its patients. Aravind eye hospitals have perfected this multitier system of expertise; indeed it is critical to their ability to deliver great care at low cost.

In education, this can mean equipping trained intermediaries who interpret the content for students, à la Digital Study Hall, with the tools to explain the content, improve their own knowledge, and assess student learning. They remain connected to the network of professional teachers; however, their tasks are largely encoded in the tools they use. The schools and colleges reduce their costs and increase their reach and impact at the same time. Similarly for research on environment and agricultural issues it can take the form of equipping the local population with the means to record and report data easily, as well as to interpret the common patterns. They become part of the network of the experts and scientists by doing so and the relationship is beneficial for both.

REIMAGINING THE ROLE OF INSTITUTIONS

In the same way, as services are taken out of specialized institutions to increase access, institutions will have to think of themselves not as isolated islands of privileged expertise, but as vital and precious elements in an ecosystem of organizations of different shapes and sizes that contribute to their evolution as well. Banks will discover new ways of doing business by observing microfinance institutions; hospitals will learn new ways of reducing costs by observing the work of clinics like the Aravind eye clinic.

The reverse is also true; the powerful analytical tools employed by banks to gauge risk will be used by microfinance institutions to be even more effective. The latest research and discoveries in the top universities will translate more quickly into breakthroughs that touch lives and create new wealth. Such symbiotic relationships already exist, for example, between the community colleges and the universities in the United States. The community colleges offer shorter, more affordable programs that end up feeding into the longer, more expensive university programs.

REIMAGINING PARTNERSHIPS

Multinational corporations (MNCs) will think of NGOs as critical partners that can help them discover the right business model. NGOs will think of businesses as essential partners in scaling up their impact and also in achieving sustainability. The entrepreneurs will realize that not all breakthroughs will be exploited effectively by MNCs; this is the case for short message service (SMS)—based applications today. Likewise, the dominant players in the PC ecosystem have been slow to adapt to the shift to mobile. Their internal constraints and those of their existing business models will limit the extent to which they will be able to play a role in the early stages of innovation. And the governments will have to be mindful about the timing and extent of policies that will be needed to create the virtuous cycle.

Solving the hard problems will require a combination of local knowledge and the global state of the art, be it in education, health care, or other relevant areas. The success of M-Pesa required an intimate partnership between international expertise in telecommunications and the deep understanding of the local context in order to succeed. Similarly a micro—health insurance scheme has been launched in Uganda to provide coverage to poor people who would normally go bankrupt when seeking care.[1] This represents the best thinking in health insurance and appropriate technology, combined with deep knowledge of local customs and needs.

India has launched a smart card—based national health insurance plan and already enrolled more than 50 million people.[2] The cost of technology is borne by the government, the technology is provided by the public sector, the health-care services are provided by the existing infrastructure, and the cardholders are free to choose the providers. This is probably the most ambitious example of a partnership between public and private, and for-profit and not-for-profit.

REIMAGINING BUSINESS MODELS

Low-cost innovation that is profitable at large volumes will be key to success. Companies are not strangers to this approach. Microsoft democratized computing by bringing it from data centers to people's homes and in the process changed how we live, work, and play. Pharmaceuticals have made really inexpensive medications available for common diseases. Online trading has brought the stock market to the masses. We are talking about the next stage in cost reduction, which will reach an even larger audience and create the new business leaders. Incumbents may not emerge as leaders in this wave and could give ground to newcomers who perfect really low-cost business models that can provide the essential functionality at affordable price points.

GE's effort at reverse innovation is an attempt, typified by Vscan, to develop products to meet the needs of emerging markets and then take them to developed markets.[3] Microsoft's Mischief Mouse and Multipoint Server and the Classmate PC from Intel are all harbingers of things to come. In fact, Microsoft has a deliberate goal in its Unlimited Potential effort to reach the next 1 billion people by 2015.[4] To achieve that, Microsoft is developing new partnerships with governments, international organizations, NGOs, educational institutions, and technology and service providers.

Traditional boundaries between sectors are also being challenged. One sees telecommunications companies such as Safaricom muscle into finance with M-Pesa to bring banking services to the masses. In response, governments are scrambling to develop policies that could either promote such efforts or restrict them. The CEO of State Bank of India commented in April 2009 at a meeting in Seattle that clearly they are interested in serving the vast majority of Indians who are currently unbanked. However, without further technology innovation and lower transaction costs they won't be able to do so.

In some cases there is cross-pollination across sectors as well. Infrastructure that is set up for microfinance could just as easily be used for health care. Grameen is experimenting with extending their microfinance network to provide health-care services.

REIMAGINING RESEARCH

To design products and services for a resource-limited environment and for people with limited skills is a very hard problem. But the rewards are tremendous in lives touched and improved. These problems have to become a legitimate field of inquiry and research in our top universities and be funded by the likes of the National Science Foundation and the National Institutes of Health (NIH). There is room for optimism as institutions like Stanford University, University of California at Berkeley, University of Washington, and many others in the United States and abroad make such efforts a part of their curriculum and research. While Microsoft Research pioneered funding in this space, the NIH has started to take the lead in mHealth,[5] as has the Gates Foundation through its Grand Challenge Explorations.[6]

Research done in low-cost diagnostics, inexpensive water purification, or affordable clean energy represents a fertile area with tremendous possibility of impact. Providing network connectivity and computing at low cost is still a challenge—especially for illiterate segments of the population. In some areas the framework has evolved rapidly. A couple of years ago, making banking affordable was about making inexpensive ATMs that could be installed in rural and remote areas.[7] Now, banking has moved to an even more affordable SMS-based model with lower transaction costs.

An added satisfaction of research in this area is the speed with which the innovations are getting commercialized, driven by the imperative of the problems to be solved. The pace is especially striking in health care, although education is not far behind. As an example, Mobisante, a start-up that makes affordable point-of-care diagnostic devices, spun out within two years of research and development in a lab in Washington University at St. Louis. The area of inquiry also appeals to our best instincts, and the evidence is clear in the high caliber of talent that is being attracted to work in this area, people who want to do well by doing good.

REIMAGINING OUR BIASES

Technology is often seen as a luxury that cash-strapped organizations such as nonprofits and social entrepreneurs can ill afford. This is a trap. In a recent article, Bill Brindley, CEO of NetHope, describes the "tyranny of the pie chart," which leads NGOs down a path of starving the efficacy of important programs in order to demonstrate low overhead to potential donors and others. In fact, however, "smart overhead" and appropriate levels of investment allow social entrepreneurs and NGOs to be much more effective in fulfilling their stated missions.[8] Just as in the case of Kiva, the technology infrastructure was key to their innovation.

There are signs that software entrepreneurs such as Voxiva and Univicity are beginning to treat the NGOs as a viable market segment and beginning to develop products that will improve their effectiveness and efficiency the same way that ICT improved the efficiency of our supply chain and manufacturing over the past two decades.

REIMAGINING PUBLIC INFRASTRUCTURE

No one questions today that clean water, electricity, waste disposal, and such are important utilities that have to be made available to everyone for the public good. Perhaps it is time to think of access to basic ICTs with the same breadth, since they can improve access to and affordability of so many more essential services. And the process of creating that infrastructure in return will create unsurpassed growth. Governments can speed up this development through a smart combination of policies, subsidies, and if needed, direct involvement to underwrite the cost of such an infrastructure. The government auctions the spectrum used by the cell phones. Hence it has a point of leverage with the telecommunications companies that bid to acquire the spectrum. Government could require that the companies use part of the spectrum for services in health care, education, and so forth, through price subsidies.

This is not as far-fetched as it sounds. Countries like South Korea have prioritized putting in broadband networks for their citizens. India and several countries in Africa set up a network of PC kiosks to serve their far-flung communities. As shared in this book, many of these struggled because of the lack of a business model. That, however, is changing now. We know that there are demands for finance, health, education, and environmental services that are being met using such an ICT network. Furthermore, they can be put together at a significantly lower cost using mobile-based as opposed to PC-based infrastructure, as was the case with Warana Unwired.

LOOKING AHEAD

We remain convinced that barring large-scale disasters that divert attention and resources to ensuring survival, the trends we cover here are real and will play out during this decade, improving lives and creating new sources of wealth. The most successful players will deeply understand the local context for which they are designing their offerings. They will tap into targeted innovation that delivers value at low cost and cultivate the right partnerships between the NGOs and the governmental agencies. They will strike a balance between the extremes of what Kentaro Toyama refers to as *technological utopianism* and treating ICT as irrelevant to those at the bottom of the economic pyramid. Some of them will become strong enough to challenge and disrupt their counterparts in the richer economies. As mentioned in the Preface, all three of us have already made choices in our own lives and careers that reflect that conviction. We encourage you to join this revolution as well.

NOTES

1. George Halvorson, *Health Care Co-Ops in Uganda: Effectively Launching Micro Health Groups in African Villages* (Portland, OR/Oakland, CA: Permanente Press, 2007).
2. Rashtriya Swasthya Bima Yojna, Ministry of Labour and Employment, www.rsby.in/.
3. GE Reports, "Vscan Pocket-Sized, Ultra-Smart Ultrasound Unveiled," www.gereports.com/vscan-pocket-sized-ultra-smart-ultrasound-unveiled, October 20, 2009.
4. Microsoft Corporation, "Corporate Citizenship," www.microsoft .com/unlimitedpotential/default.mspx, 2010.
5. 36th Annual International Conference Global Health: www.globalhealth .org/conference_2009 (accessed March 7, 2010).
6. Grand Challenges in Global Health, "Topic: Create Low-Cost Cell Phone-Based Applications for Priority Global Health Conditions," www.grandchallenges.org/MeasureHealthStatus/Topics/CellPhone-Apps/Pages/Round5.aspx, (March 2010).
7. Tenet: The Telecommunications and Computer Networking Group, "Partners," www.tenet.res.in/Partners/index.php (accessed March 2, 2010).
8. William Brindley, "The Tyranny of the Pie Chart: How Unrealistic Operating Budgets Starve NGOs and Prevent Optimal Performance," *Huffington Post*, www.huffingtonpost.com/william-brindley/the-tyranny-of-the-pie-ch_b_395138.html, December 16, 2009.

REFERENCES

Accenture (2007). "Outsourcing: AMREF and Accenture: Working Together to Launch an Unprecedented E-Learning Initiative to Address a Critical Nursing Shortage in Kenya," www.accenture.com/NR/rdonlyres/84E3B47A-07E8-44D2-97BD-AA5EC4089E3B/0/AMREF.pdf.

Ahmad, A. "Management Information Systems (MIS) for Microfinance," The First Microfinance Bank Ltd., Pakistan. www.bwtp.org/pdfs/arcm/5Ahmad.pdf. Accessed June 2008.

AMREF. "Upgrading 20,000 Nurses in Kenya," www.amref.org/what-we-do/upgrading-20000-nurses-in-kenya. Accessed August 26, 2010.

Andrews, E. (2009). "A 'Positivo' Milestone for Intel-Powered Classmate PCs!" Technology@Intel, http://blogs.intel.com/technology/2009/06/a_positivo_milestone_for_intel.php.

Angrist, J., and V. Lavy (2002). "New Evidence on Classroom Computers and Pupil Learning," *Economic Journal* 112(482): 735–765.

ApproTEC: www.approtec.org.

ApproTEC (2005). "Winner's Statement," *Fast Company*, www.fastcompany.com/social/2005/statements/approtec.html. Accessed July 14, 2010.

Aravind Eye Care System: www.aravind.org.

Arunachalam, S. (2003). "Information for Research in Developing Countries: Information Technology, a Friend or Foe?" *International Information & Library Review*, 35(2): 133–147.

Asian Development Bank (ADB). "Microfinance Development Strategy." www.adb.org/Documents/Policies/Microfinance/microfinance0100 .asp?p=microfnc. Accessed June 2008.

Attewell, P., and J. Battle (1999). "Home Computers and School Performance," *Information Society* 15(1): 1–10.

Baldacci, E., B. Clements, Q. Cui, and S. Gupta (2005). "What Does It Take to Help the Poor?" *Finance and Development* 42(2).

Banerjee, A. V., S. Cole, et al. (2007). "Remedying Education: Evidence from Two Randomized Experiments in India," *Quarterly Journal of Economics* 122(3): 1235–1264.

Bangelstorff, A. (November 2007). "Use Your Mobile Phone for Marketing," *The Organic Farmer*, 30.

Barrow, L., L. Markman, et al. (2007). "Technology's Edge: The Educational Benefits of Computer-Aided Instruction," Federal Reserve Bank of Chicago, WP 2007-17.

Bashshur, R. (1980). *Technology Serves the People: The Story of a Cooperative Telemedicine Project by NASA, the Indian Health Service and the Papago People.* Washington, DC: National Aeronautics and Space Administration.

Basu, D., and W. Brimley. (September 26, 2006). "Disaster Relief" (whitepaper). www.nethope.org/images/uploads/casestudies/DisasterRelief.pdf.

Becker, H. J. (2000). "Who's Wired and Who's Not: Children's Access to and Use of Computer Technology," *Future of Children* 10(2): 44–75.

Best, M. (2008). *Reflections on (Un)sustainability: The Sustainable Access in Rural Internet (SARI) Project Nearly One Decade On.* Proceedings of SLPTMD Conference: Confronting the Challenge of Technology for Development: Experiences from the BRICS. University of Oxford.

Beveridge, M., A. Howard, K. Burton, and W. Holder (2003). "The Ptolemy Project: A Scalable Model for Delivering Health Information in Africa," *British Medical Journal* 327(7418), 790–793.

Bhandari, A., M. Ibrahim, and J.S. Sandhu (2004). *Remote Eye Care Delivery via Rural Information Kiosks* (white paper). Berkeley, CA: University of California.

Bhatnagar, S. and Dewan, A., Moreno Torres, M., and Kanungo, P. (2004). "Grameen Telecom: The Village Phone Program: Empowerment Case Studies," Indian Institute of Management and World Bank. poverty.worldbank .org/sites/14648_grameen_web.pdf.

Bill and Melinda Gates Foundation. "Diconsa: Bringing Financial Services to the Rural Poor in Mexico." www.gatesfoundation.org/grantee-profiles/Pages/ diconsa-financial-services-for-the-rural-poor.aspx. Accessed August 26, 2010.

Bladin, P. (Spring 2007). "Improving Microfinance through Telecommuni-cations," *ESR Review* 9(1). www.grameenfoundation.org/pubdownload/ ~pubid=44.

Bosch, A. (1997). *Interactive Radio Instruction: Twenty-Three Years of Improving Education Quality.* Washington, DC: World Bank Group.

Bridges.org: www.bridges.org.

Bruns, B., A. Mingat, and R. Rakotomalala (2003). *Achieving Universal Primary Education by 2015: A Chance for Every Child*. The World Bank, http://go .worldbank.org/F30T33DI80.

David Burela (2008). "SOAK: Smart Operational Agriculture Kit." http:// davidburela.files.wordpress.com/2008/05/soak-executive-summary.pdf.

Careem, M., R. De Silva, C. De Silva, L. Raschid, and S. Weerawarana. (2006), "Sahana: Overview of a Disaster Management System." Proceedings of the International Conference on Information and Automation, Colombo, Sri Lanka.

Cecchini, S., and M. Raina. (April 2002). "Warana: The Case of an Indian Rural Community Adopting ICT," *Information Technology in Developing Countries*, 12(1).

Center for the Study of Financial Innovation (2008). "Microfinance Banana Skins 2008 Report."

Centers for Disease Control and Prevention (2005). "EpiInfo." www.cdc.gov/ epiinfo.

Chandrasekhar, C. P. (March–April 2005). "ICT and Rural Livelihoods," *Mainstreaming ICTs* 2(2): 32–35.

Chandrasekhar, C. P., and J. Ghosh (2001). "Information and Communication Technologies and Health in Low Income Countries: The Potential and the Constraints," *Bull World Health Organ* 79(9): 850–855.

Chandru, V., V.L. Deshpande, S. Garg, R. Harirahan, S. Manohar, M. Mathias, and V. Vinay (2001). *The Simputer: Radical Simplicity for Universal Access*. Bangalore, India: The Simputer Trust.

Chesbrough, H. (2003). *Open Innovation: The New Imperative for Creating and Profiting from Technology*. Cambridge, MA: Harvard Business School Press.

Chesbrough, H., and S. Ahern, M. Finn, and S. Guerraz (May 01, 2006). "Business Models for Technology in the Developing World: The Role of Non-Governmental Organizations." *California Management Review* 338.

Chesbrough, H., and R. Rosenbloom (2002). "The Role of the Business Model in Capturing Value from Innovation: Evidence from Xerox Corporation's Technology Spinoff Companies," *Industrial and Corporate Change* 11(3): 529–555.

Christensen, C. (1997). *The Innovator's Dilemma: When New Technologies Cause Great Firms to Fail*. Cambridge, MA: Harvard Business School Press.

Christensen, C., J. H. Grossman, and J. Hwang (2008). *The Innovator's Prescription: A Disruptive Solution for Health Care*. New York: McGraw-Hill.

Christensen, C., M. B. Horn, and C. W. Johnson (2008). *Disrupting Class: How Disruptive Innovation Will Change the Way the World Learns*. New York: McGraw Hill.

Christensen, C., and M. E Raynor (2003). *The Innovator's Solution: Creating and Sustaining Successful Growth*. Cambridge, MA: Harvard Business School Press.

Chitrangada, C. (December 30, 2006). "From IIT Lab, Engineers SMS Help to Farmers." *Hindustan Times*. www.hindustantimes.com/StoryPage/Print/ 196823.aspx.

Cohen, N. (June 2001). "What Works: Grameen Telecom's Village Phones," www.wri.org/publication/what-works-grameen-telecoms-village-phones.

Colle, R., and L. Yonggong (2002) "ICT Capacity-Building for Development and Poverty Alleviation: Enhancing the Role of Agricultural Universities in China." http://zoushoku.narc.affrc.go.jp/ADR/AFITA/afita/afita-conf/2002/part1/p067.pdf.

Consultative Group to Assist the Poor (CGAP): www.cgap.org/p/site/c.

Consultative Group to Assist the Poor (CGAP). *Financial Access 2009: Measuring Access to Financial Services around the World*, The World Bank. www.cgap.org/gm/document-1.9.38735/FA2009.pdf. Accessed October 2009.

Consultative Group to Assist the Poor (CGAP). "Information Systems: Frequently Asked Questions." www.cgap.org/gm/document-1.9.2017/IS_Technology_FAQs.pdf. Accessed February 2010.

Cracknell, D. (2004). "Electronic Banking for the Poor: Panacea, Potential, and Pitfalls," *Small Enterprise Development* 15(4): 8–24.

Cuban, L. (2001). *Oversold and Underused: Computers in the Classroom*. Cambridge, MA: Harvard University Press.

Currion, P., C. De Silva, and V. De Walle (March 2007). "Open Source Software for Disaster Management," *Communications of the ACM* 50(3).

Cutler, D., and M. McClellan (2001). "Is Technological Change in Medicine Worth It?" *Health Affairs* 20(5): 11–29.

Dailey, J. (2006). "Microfinance Needs a Common Platform for Access to Capital and Scalable Operational Systems." In *Electronic Banking with the Poor*, edited by Stuart Mathison. Foundation for Development Cooperation.

Daley-Harris, S., J. Keenan, and K. Speerstra (2007). *Our Day to End Poverty: 24 Ways You Can Make a Difference*. San Francisco: Berrett-Koehler Publishers.

Deaton, A. (2003). "Health, Inequality and Economic Development," *Journal of Economic Literature* 41(1): 113–158.

Dees, G. (2001). "The Meaning of Social Entrepreneurship," www.caseatduke.org/documents/dees_sedef.pdf. Accessed October 2008.

Demirguc-Kunt, A., T. Beck, and P. Honohan (2008). "Finance for All? Policies and Pitfalls in Expanding Access," The International Bank of Reconstruction and Development—The World Bank. Full text accessible at www.worldbank.org.

Demiris, G. (2004). Preface. In G. Demiris (Ed.), *E-Health: Current Status and Future Trends* (Vol. 106, p. 145). Washington DC: IOS Press.

Digital Green. "Overview," http://research.microsoft.com/en-us/um/india/projects/digitalgreen/default.htm. Accessed July 2008.

Digital Study Hall: http://dsh.cs.washington.edu.

Dossani, R., D. Misra, and R. Jhaveri (November 2005). "Enabling ICT for Rural India," Asia-Pacific Research Center, Stanford University.

Duflo, E. (2004). *Scaling Up and Evaluation. Annual World Bank Conference on Development* Washington DC: World Bank/Oxford University Press, pp. 341–369.

Eduinnova: www.eduinnova.com.

Ehrmann, S. C., S.W. Gilbert, and F. McMartin (2006). "Factors Affecting the Adoption of Faculty-Developed Academic Software: A Study of Five iCampus Projects," TLT Group.

Ferraz, C. C., R. Fonseca, J. Pal, and M. Shah (May 2004). "Computing for Social Inclusion in Brazil: A Study of the CDI and Other Initiatives," *First UCB-UNIDO Bridging the Divide Conference*. Berkeley, CA, UNIDO.

Firpo, J. (2005). "Banking the Unbanked: Technology's Role in Delivering Accessible Financial Services to the Poor." www.gdrc.org/icm/govern/banking-unbanked.pdf.

Fisher, M. (Winter 2006). "Income is Development: KickStart's Pumps Help Kenyan Farmers Transition to a Cash Economy," *Innovations* 1(1).

Flannery, M. (Winter/Spring 2007). "Kiva and the Birth of Person to Person Microfinance," *Innovations* 2(1-2).

Flores, F., M. Flores, and C. Spinosa (Summer 2003). "Developing Productive Customers in Emerging Markets," *California Management Review* 45.

Fonseca, R., and J. Pal (2004). "Computing Devices for All: Creating and Selling the Low Cost Computer." http://tier.cs.berkeley.edu/docs/ict4d06/computing_devices_all-jp_rf.pdf. Accessed March 2007.

Food and Agriculture Organization (FAO) (2005). "Bridging the Rural Digital Divide: e-Agriculture." www.fao.org/rdd/doc/e-agriculture%2014-10-051.pdf.

Fox, T. (2004). "Corporate Social Responsibility and Development: In Quest of an Agenda," *Development* 47(4): 29–36.

Gelb, E. (2005). "Adoption in Agriculture and Rural Development: A *5th EFITA/WCCA Conference* Theme Report."

Global Health (2009), www.globalhealth.org/conference_2009/.

Graham, L., M. Zimmerman, D. Vassallo, V. Patterson, P. Swinfen, R. Swinfen, et al. (2003). "Telemedicine: The Way Ahead for Medicine in the Developing World," *Tropical Doctor*, 33(1): 36–38.

Grameen Foundation: www.grameenfoundation.org.

Grand Challenges in Global Health (March 2010). "Topic: Create Low-Cost Cell Phone-Based Applications for Priority Global Health Conditions." www.grandchallenges.org/MeasureHealthStatus/Topics/CellPhoneApps/Pages/Round5.aspx.

Haddad, W. D., and A. Draxler (2002). *Technologies for Education: Potentials, Parameters, and Prospects*. Paris: UNESCO and Academy for Educational Development.

Halvorson, G. (2007). *Health Care Co-Ops in Uganda: Effectively Launching Micro Health Groups in African Villages*. Oakland, CA/Portland, OR: Permanente Press.

Hammond, A. L., W. J. Kramer, R. S. Katz, J. T. Tran, and C. Walker (2007). *The Next 4 Billion: Market Size and Business Strategy at the Base of the Pyramid*. World Resources Institute and International Finance Corporation/World Bank Group.

Hammond, A. L., and C. K. Prahalad (May–June 2004). "Selling to the Poor," *Foreign Policy*.

Hanson, K., and P. Berman (1998). "Private Healthcare Provision in Developing Countries: A Preliminary Analysis of Levels and Composition," *Health Policy and Planning* 13(3): 195–211.

Harkin, G. "ICT Adoption as an Agricultural Information Dissemination Tool: An Historical Perspective." http://departments.agri.huji.ac.il/economics/gelb-harkin-3.pdf. Accessed August 26, 2010.

Hart, S. L. (2005). *Capitalism at the Crossroads*. Upper Saddle River, NJ: Wharton School Publishing.

Hawkins, R. J. (2004). "Ten Lessons for ICT and Education in the Developing World," *Global Information Technology Report 2005*.

Heath, M., and J. Ravitz (2001). "Teaching, Learning and Computing: What Teachers Say," *ED-MEDIA 2001, World Conference on Educational Multimedia, Hypermedia and Telecommunications*.

Heeks, R. (2002). "Information Systems and Developing Countries: Failure, Success, and Local Improvisations," *The Information Society* 18: 101–112.

Hepp, P., E. Hinostroza, E. Laval, and L. Rehbein (2004). *Technology in Schools: Education, ICT and the Knowledge Society*. World Bank, www.worldbank.org/education/pdf/ICT_report_oct04a.pdf.

Herring, D. (January 29, 2001). "Precision Farming." NASA Earth Observatory. http://earthobservatory.nasa.gov/Study/PrecisionFarming/precision_farming.html.

Hess, D., N. Rogovsky, and T. Dunfee (2002). "The Next Wave of Corporate Community Involvement: Corporate Social Initiatives," *California Management Review* 44(2): 110–125.

Highfield, R. (January 30, 2008)."Larry Brilliant, of Google.org: Internet 'Is Pandemic Early Warning System," *Telegraph* online edition.

Hillman, A. L., and E. Jenker (2004). "Educating Children in Poor Countries," *International Monetary Fund*.

Hughes, H. and S. Lonie (2007). "M-Pesa: Mobile Money for the 'Unbanked.' Turning cell phone into 24-hour tellers in Kenya," *Innovations*, Winter/Spring.

IBM: www.ibm.com.

iCampus: The MIT-Microsoft Alliance (March 29, 2005). "iLabs: Internet Access to Real Labs—Anywhere, Anytime," http://icampus.mit.edu/ilabs.

iCampus: The MIT–Microsoft Alliance (January 8, 2007). "MIT iCampus 1999–2006," http://icampus.mit.edu.

Immelt, J. R., V. Govindarajan, and C. Trimble (October 2009). "How GE Is Disrupting Itself," *Harvard Business Review*.

India Disaster Resource Network: www.idrn.gov.in.

Intel Corporation: www.intel.com.

International Development Enterprises (India): www.ide-india.org/ide/index1.shtml. Accessed July 14, 2010.

IRIN (June 3, 2009). "Nigeria: Childbirth Still Deadly," www.irinnews.org.

Islam, Y. M., M. Ashraf, et al. (2005). "Mobile Telephone Technology as a Distance Learning Tool," *ICEIS*.

Ivatury, G. (December 2004). *Harnessing Technology to Transform Financial Services for the Poor*. ITDG Publishing. www.microfinancegateway.com/content/article/detail/25234.

Ivatury, G. (January 2006). "Using Technology to Build Inclusive Financial Systems," CGAP Focus Note No. 32.

Ivatury, G., and I. Mas (April 2008). "The Early Experience with Branchless Banking," CGAP Focus Note No. 46. www.cgap.org/gm/document-1.9.2640/FocusNote_46.pdf.

Ivatury, G., and N. Pasricha (April 2005). "Helping to Improve Donor Effectiveness in Microfinance," Consultative Group for the Poor (CGAP) Donor Brief No. 23.

James, J. (2001). "Low-Cost Computing and Related Ways of Overcoming the Global Digital Divide," *Journal of Information Science* 27(6): 385–392.

Jamison, D. T. (1978). *Radio for Education and Development*. Beverly Hills, CA: Sage Publications.

Jenkins, R. (2005). "Globalization, Corporate Social Responsibility and Poverty," *International Affairs* 81(3): 525–540.

Kam, M., D. Ramachandran, et al. (2007). "Localized Iterative Design for Language Learning in Underdeveloped Regions: The PACE Framework," *Proceedings of the Sigchi Conference on Human Factors in Computing Systems*, pp. 1097–1106.

Karamchandani, A., M. Kubzansky, and P. Frandano (March 2009). *Emerging Market, Emerging Models: Market Based Solutions to the Challenges of Global Poverty*. Monitor Group.

Ketley, R., and B. Duminy. "Meeting the Challenge: The Impact of Changing Technology on Microfinance Institutions (MFIs)," MicroSave Briefing Note No. 21. www.microsave.org/briefing_notes/bn21-impact-of-changing-technology-on-microfinance. Accessed August 26, 2010.

KickStart: www.kickstart.org.

Kirkpatrick, H., and L. Cuban (1998). "Computers Make Kids Smarter—Right?" *Technos Quarterly for Education and Technology* 7(2): 1–10.

Kiva: www.kiva.org.

Lazear, E. P. (2001). "Educational Production," *Quarterly Journal of Economics* 116(3): 777–803.

Leary, J., and Z. Berge. (2006). "Trends and Challenges of eLearning in National and International Agricultural Development," *International Journal of Education and Development using Information and Communication Technology* 2(2): 51–59.

Leclercq, F. (2005). *The Relationship between Educational Expenditures and Outcomes: Document De Travail*. Paris: DIAL (Developpement Institutions et Analyses de Long Terme).

Librero, F. (2007). "Uses of the Cell Phone for Education in the Philippines and Mongolia," *Distance Education* 28(2): 231–244.

Lopez, A. D., and C. C. Murray (1998). "The Global Burden of Disease, 1990–2020," *Natural Medicine*, 4(11): 1241–1243.

Lumpkin, J. R., and M. S. Richards (2002). "Transforming the Public Health Information Infrastructure," *Health Affairs* 21(6): 45.

Machin, S., S. McNally, et al. (2005). *Investing in Technology: Is There a Payoff in Schools?* London: Centre for the Economics of Education.

Maru A. (2002). "A Normative Model for Agricultural Research Information Systems." http://zoushoku.narc.affrc.go.jp/ADR/AFITA/afita/afita-conf/2002/part0/p019.pdf.

Maru, A., and K. Ehrle (2003). "Building a Framework for ICT Use in Agricultural Research and Development: Is the North Different from the South?," *EFITA 2003 Conference*, July 5–9, 2003, Debrecen, Hungary.

Mas, I., and H. Siedek (2008). "Banking through Networks of Retail Agents," CGAP Focus Note No. 47.

Massachusetts Institute of Technology. "MIT Open Courseware." http://ocw.mit.edu/index.htm. Accessed August 26, 2010.

Mathison, Stuart (2005). "Increasing the Outreach and Sustainability of Microfinance through ICT Innovation." Available through the Foundation for Development Cooperation. www.fdc.org.au.

Matthews, L. (2009) "Can Technology Better the Lives of the Poor?" *Good Stories*, http://goodstories.wordpress.com/2009/07/15/can-technology-better-the-lives-of-the-poor.

Microsoft: www.microsoft.com.

Microsoft. "Global Partnerships." www.microsoft.com/about/corporatecitizenship.

Microsoft. "Unlimited Potential." www.microsoft.com/about/corporate citizenship/en-us/about/unlimited-potential. Accessed August 26, 2010.

Microsoft (January 21, 2004). "Medical Diagnostic and Treatment Software Holds Potential to Save Lives and Improve Patient Care Worldwide," microsoft.com/presspass/feautures/2004/jan04/01-21NxOpinion.mspx.

Microsoft (2009). "Microsoft Hosted Online Service to Help Flu Sufferers Seek the Right Medical Help," Microsoft News Center, October 15, www.microsoft.com/presspass/features/2009/oct09/10ç15flualert.mspx.

Microsoft (2010). "Microsoft Imagine Us." www.imagineusgulf.com.

Microsoft Research: research.microsoft.com.

Microsoft Research (2007). "The Classroom of Tomorrow, Built with Today's Technology." http://research.microsoft.com/en-us/collaboration/papers/chile.pdf.

Microsoft Research (2007). "HealthLine Offers Speech-Based Access to Medical Information." http://research.microsoft.com/en-us/collaboration/papers/carnegie_mellon.pdf.

Microsoft Research (2008). "CellScope Could Offer Low-Cost Portable Options for Disease Diagnosis." http://research.microsoft.com/en-us/collaboration/focus/health/cellscope.pdf.

Microsoft Research (2008). "Mobile Language-Learning Tools Help Pave the Way to Literacy." http://research.microsoft.com/en-us/collaboration/papers/berkeley.pdf.

Microsoft Research (2008). "Portable Diagnostic Device Can Help Save Lives." http://research.microsoft.com/en-us/collaboration/papers/hyderabad.pdf.

Microsoft Research (2008). "Ultrasound Imaging More Portable, Affordable with USB-Based Probes." http://research.microsoft.com/en-us/collaboration/focus/health/msr_ultrasound.pdf.

Minkler, M. (Ed.). (1997). *Community Organizing & Community Building for Health.* New Brunswick, NJ: Rutgers State University Press.

Mohanty S., H. Karelia, and R. Issar. (2005). "ICT for Disaster Risk Reduction: The Indian Experience," Ministry of Home Affairs, National Disaster Management Division.

Moni, M. (March–April 2005). "ICT for Sustainable Rural Livelihoods," *Mainstreaming ICTs*, 2(2): 35–38.

Mungai, W. (2005). "Using ICTs for Poverty Reduction and Environmental Protection in Kenya: The 'M-vironment' Approach." In *A Developing Connection: Bridging the Policy Gap between the Information Society and Sustainable Development,* edited by Terri Willard and Maja Andjelkovic, 43–85. International Institute for Sustainable Development, 2005.

Murphy, D. (August 13, 2009). "NMA Global Campaigns." *New Media Age,* www.nma.co.uk/features/global-campaigns/3003382.article.

Nasikye, E. (August 24, 2008). "Mobile Telephony Makes a Difference in Livelihoods," http://mobileactive.org/Mobile+Telephony+Makes+a+Difference+in+Livelihoods.

Nielsen, J. (2000). *Designing Web Usability.* Indianapolis, IN: New Riders.

n-Logue: www.tenet.res.in/Partners/index.php.

Novoy-Hildesley, J. (2010). "By the Grace of Innovation. Special Edition for Tech4Society: A Celebration of Ashoka-Lemelson Fellows," *Innovations.* Cambridge MIT Press.

Organisation for Economic Co-Operation and Development (OECD) (2009). *Education at a Glance 2009: OECD Indicators.* Paris, France.

Pakenham-Walsh, N., C. Priestley, and R. Smith (1997). "Meeting the Information Needs of Health Workers in Developing Countries," *British Medical Journal* 314 (7074): 90.

Pal, J. (2006). "Early-Stage Practicalities of Implementing Computer Aided Education: Experience from India," *Fourth IEEE International Workshop on Technology for Education in Developing Countries.*

Pal, J., M. Lakshmanan, and K. Toyama (December 2007). "'My Child Will Be Respected': Parental Perspectives on Computers in Rural India," *Second International Conference on Information Technologies and Development, IEEE Conference Proceedings* 2: 168–177.

Pal, J., U. S. Pawar, E. Brewer, and K. Toyama. (2006). "The Case for Multi-User Design for Computer Aided Learning in Developing Regions," *Proceedings of the 15th International Conference on World Wide Web,* pp. 781–789.

Papert, S. (1993). *The Children's Machine: Rethinking School in the Age of the Computer.* New York: Basic Books.

Parikh, T. S. (2004). *Rural Microfinance Service Delivery: Gaps, Inefficiencies and Emerging Solutions.* Department of Computer Science, University of Washington. www.fdc.org.au/Electronic%20Banking%20with%20the%20Poor/3%20Parikh.pdf.

Parikh, T. S. (May 2006). "Rural Microfinance Service Delivery: Gaps, Ineff-iciencies and Emerging Solutions." International Conference on Information and Communication Technologies and Development. ICTD 2006, 223–232.

Partners in Health (2010). "PIH Model Online: Electronic Medical Records (EMR)." http://model.pih.org/electronic_medical_records.

Patra, R., J. Pal, S. Nedevschi, M. Plauche, and U. Pawar (December 2007). "Usage Models of Classroom Computing in Developing Regions," Second International Conference on Information Technologies and Development, IEEE Conference Proceedings, Bangalore.

Pawar, U. S., J. Pal, and K. Toyama (2006). "Multiple Mice for Computers in Education in Developing Countries," ICTD 2006 Conference Program Proceedings, May 25–26, 2006.

Pedersen, M. and D. Del Ser (June 17, 2009). "Smartphones and Emerging Markets: A New Technology Revolution?" *Columbia Business School Public Offering.*

Pfizer: www.pfizer.com.

Pop!Tech. "Project Masiluleke." www.poptech.org/project_m. Accessed August 26, 2010.

Porteous. D. (May 2006). "Banking and the Last Mile: Technology and the Distribution of Financial Services in Developing Countries." Report available through the World Bank. www.worldbank.org.

Porteous, D. (2006). "The Enabling Environment for Mobile Banking in Africa." Report commissioned by DFID. Available through Bankable Frontier Asso-ciates. www.bankablefrontier.com/assets/ee.mobil.banking.report.v3.1.pdf.

PR Newswire (October 7, 2009). "Microsoft Launches Online H1N1 Flu Response Center to Support Consumers." www.prnewswire.com/news-releases/microsoft-launches-online-h1n1-flu-response-center-to-support-consumers-63664347.html.

Prahalad, C. K (2004). *The Fortune at the Bottom of the Pyramid.* Upper Saddle River, NJ: Wharton School Publishing.

Prahalad, C. K., and A. Hammond (2002). "Serving the World's Poor, Profitably," *Harvard Business Review* 80(9): 48–58.

Prahalad, C. K., and S. L. Hart (2002). "The Fortune at the Bottom of the Pyramid," *strategy+business* 26.

Quick, J. D. (2003). "Ensuring Access to Essential Medicines in the Developing Countries: A Framework for Action," *Clinical Pharmacology & Therapeutics* 73(4): 279–283.

Rao, M. (2004). "Micro-Finance and ICTs: Exploring Mutual Benefits and Synergy," Orbicom, www.orbicom.ca/in_focus/columns/en/archives/2004_avril.html.

Rashtriya Swasthya Bima Yojna, Ministry of Labour and Employment, www.rsby.in/.

Rickman, D., J. C. Luvall, J. Shaw, P. Mask, D. Kissel, and D. Sullivan (November 2003). "Precision Agriculture: Changing the Face of Farming," *GeoTimes.*

Rothenberg-Aalami, J. and J. Pal (2005). "Rural Telecenter Impact Assessments and the Political Economy of ICT for Development (ICT4D)." Berkeley Roundtable for the International Economy (BRIE) Working Paper 164.

Russell, S. (2004). "The Economic Burden of Illness for Households in Developing Countries: A Review of Studies Focusing on Malaria, Tuberculosis, and Human Immunodeficiency Virus/Acquired Immunodeficiency Syndrome," *American Journal of Tropical Medicine and Hygiene* 71(2 suppl.): 147–155.

Sachs, J. (2005). *The End of Poverty: Economic Possibilities for Our Time.* New York: Penguin.

Sachs, J. (2008). *Common Wealth: Economics for a Crowded Planet.* New York: Penguin.

Salomon, G. (1984). "Television Is 'Easy' and Print Is 'Tough': The Differences in Investment of Mental Effort in Learning as a Function of Perceptions and Attributions," *Journal of Educational Psychology* 76(4): 647–658.

Sahana: www.sahanafoundation.org.

SchoolNet Africa: www.schoolnetafrica.org.

Scott, T., M. Cole, and M. Engle (1992). "Computers and Education: A Cultural Constructivist Perspective." *Review of Research in Education* 18: 191–251.

Shaik M., A. Jhamtani, and D. Rao (January 2004). "Information and Communication Technology in Agricultural Development: A Comparative Analysis of Three Projects from India," Agricultural Research and Extension Network, Network Paper No. 135.

SKS India: www.sksindia.com.

Srinivasan, K. "The KioskNet Project." http://blizzard.cs.uwaterloo.ca/tetherless/index.php/KioskNet. Accessed July 14, 2010.

Stanisljevic, Z. (April 8, 2009). "Microcapital Story: CGAP and WIZZIT Collaborate to Expand Mobile Technology Services to Provide Branchless Banking to Poor Citizens in Rural South Africa," Microcapital.org.

Strasburger, V. C. (1986). "Does Television Affect Learning and School Performance?" *Pediatrician* 13(2–3): 141–147.

Tan-Torres Edejer, T. (September 30, 2000). "Disseminating Health Information in Developing Countries: The Role of the Internet," *BMJ* 321(7264): 797–800.

TechnoServe. "TechnoServe Coffee Initiative." www.technoserve.org/assets/documents/jan2009coffeeinitiativefactsheet.pdf. Accessed October 2009.

Telemedicine: A Guide to Assessing Telecommunications in Healthcare. (1996). Washington, DC: Committee on Evaluating Clinical Applications of Telemedicine, U.S. Institute of Medicine.

Text To Change: www.texttochange.org.

Thulasi Bai, V., V. Murali, R. Kim, and S.K. Srivatsa (June 30, 2007). "Teleophthalmology-Based Rural Eye Care in India," *Telemedicine and e-Health* 13(3).

Trucano, M. (2005). *Knowledge Maps: ICTs in Education.* Washington DC: World Bank.

UNESCO (2002). *Information and Communication Technology in Education: A Curriculum for Schools and Programme of Teacher Development.* Paris: UNESCO Division of Higher Education.

UNESCO (2005). *Children Out of School: Measuring Exclusion from Primary Education.* Montreal: UNESCO Institute for Statistics.

UNESCO (2006). *Literacy for Life: EFA Global Monitoring Report*. Paris: UNESCO Publishing.

UNESCO (2008). *Education for All by 2015: Will We Make It? EFA Global Monitoring Report*. Paris: Oxford University Press (UNESCO Publishing).

UNESCO (2010). *Education for All (EFA) Report*. Geneva: UNESCO.

United Nations. (2005). *Declaration of Helsinki: Ethical Principles for Medical Research Involving Human Subjects*. World Medical Association.

UNO (1948). *Universal Declaration of Human Rights*. General Assembly Resolution 217.

UNO (2000). *Millennium Development Goals*. United Nations Millennium Declaration: General Assembly Resolution 55/2.

Ushahidi. "About Ushahidi." www.ushahidi.com/about. Accessed March 3, 2010.

Vestergaard Frandsen: "Lifestraw." www.vestergaard-frandsen.com/lifestraw.

Vital Wave Consulting (2009). *mHealth for Development: The Opportunity of Mobile Technology for Healthcare in the Developing World*. Washington, DC and Berkshire, UK: UN Foundation-Vodafone Foundation Partnership.

Vodafone Corporation: www.vodafone.com.

Voxiva (2005): www.voxiva.com.

Wang, X., T. Wang, et al. (2002). "Usage of Instructional Materials in High Schools: Analyses of NELS Data," *Annual Meeting of American Educational Research Association*, New Orleans.

Wenglinsky, H. (2008). *Does It Compute? The Relationship between Educational Technology and Student Achievement in Mathematics*, Princeton, NJ: Educational Testing Service (ETS).

WHO (1948). *World Health Organization Constitution*. Geneva: World Health Organization.

WHO (2001). *United Nations Millennium Action Plan: Health InterNetwork*. www.healthinternetwork.net/src/millenium.php.

WHO (2005). "HealthMapper." www.who.int/health_mapping/tools/healthmapper/en/.

The World Bank: www.worldbank.org/education.

The World Bank (2005). *Financing Information and Communication Infrastructure Needs in the Developing World: Public and Private Roles*. Washington DC: Global Information and Communication Technologies Department, The World Bank.

The World Bank (2010). "Microfinance: At a Glance." http://web.worldbank.org/WBSITE/EXTERNAL/NEWS/0,,contentMDK:20433592~menuPK:34480~pagePK:64257043~piPK:437376~theSitePK:4607,00.html.

World Wildlife Fund (2008). *Living Planet*. Switzerland: World Wildlife Fund.

Wulfson, M. (2001). "The Ethics of Corporate Social Responsibility and Philanthropic Ventures," *Journal of Business Ethics* 29(1): 135–144.

Yamamoto, C. (2004). *Output-Based Aid in Health: Reaching the Poor through Public–Private Partnership*. Washington DC: World Bank.

Zhang, D., and P. U. Unschuld (November 2008). "China's Barefoot Doctor: Past, Present, and Future," *Lancet* 372(9653): 1865–1867.

INDEX

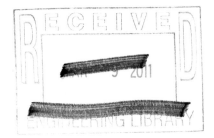